Praise for the author's fir
*A 1,000-Mile Walk on the Beach*,
about her 2009 trek around the perimeter of Lake Michigan:

"In her walk, Loreen Niewenhuis accomplished what many of us have only daydreamed about. Her adventure is told with verve and boldness, and she is a clear-eyed observer of the lake and its beautiful and some-times ravaged shore."
– Jerry Dennis, author, *The Living Great Lakes*

"Niewenhuis took a rather long stroll . . . in fact, a 1,000-mile hike . . . [and] has memorialized the experience in a fascinating book."
– *Chicago Sun-Times*

"Loreen Niewenhuis is a wonder, for her vision, accomplishment, and ability to engage and excite her audience. We are all challenged by her citing an adventurous goal and achieving it."
– Barbara Siepker, Cottage Book Shop

"*A 1,000-Mile Walk on the Beach* was a source of inspiration to our customers. It speaks authentically about the challenge of the trek around Lake Michigan and the joys of becoming more intimately acquainted with the lake we love. With sensitivity and humor, Loreen's writings give a gentle message to the reader to care for the great natural resource we have here."
– Pam & Dick Haferman, Black River Books

"*A 1,000-Mile Walk on the Beach* is a great way to relive moments spent on Lake Michigan and its shoreline – and an insight into what lies in the mysterious areas we are unable to access and explore."
– Linda Brandt, "Any Day With Books" Book Club

For more about Loreen Niewenhuis's walking adventures, writings, and availability as a speaker, visit:

www.LakeTrek.com

# A 1,000-Mile Great Lakes Walk

## One Woman's Trek
## Along the Shorelines
## of All Five Great Lakes

by

## Loreen Niewenhuis

*"Life should be an adventure!"*

CRICKHOLLOW BOOKS

Crickhollow Books is an imprint of Great Lakes Literary, LLC, of Milwaukee, Wisconsin, an independent press working to create books of lasting quality.

Our titles are available from your favorite bookstore.
For a complete catalog of all our titles or to place special orders:

www.CrickhollowBooks.com

*A 1,000-Mile Great Lakes Walk*
© 2013, Loreen Niewenhuis

Cover photograph is by Philip Rugel.

Original Trade Softcover

ISBN-13: 978-1-933987-21-7
(ISBN-10: 1-933987-21-9)

# Contents

# Introduction

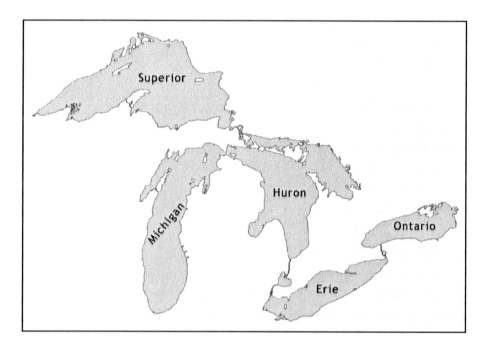

## The reasons

Near the middle of my last adventure, a 1,000-mile walk around the perimeter of Lake Michigan, I began to call it "The Adventure of a Lifetime." Then, as I got close to the finish, a thought began to gnaw at me: *This can't be the only one. . . . This is too much fun. . . .*

On my journey, I had learned so much about the lake, met many fascinating people, and expanded my sense of self and what I could accomplish. And so, even as I was finishing my first 1,000-mile hike, the seed was planted to do another. The *where* and *when* hadn't yet been determined, but a new adventure was there in the future, waiting for me.

My first hike had given me a step-by-step sense of the true size of Lake Michigan. Encircling the world's fifth largest lake on foot made me even more captivated with how that huge body of water connected with the even larger system known as the Great Lakes. The vastness of this vital collection of fresh water is astonishing; the amount of water contained in these lakes so enormous it is measured in *cubic miles.*

I also contemplated the relationship of my home state – Michigan – to that system as I walked. We Michiganders are peninsular people. Two peninsulas form our distinctive state. The mitten forms the Lower Peninsula, and the Upper Peninsula hovers above it, almost touching the top of the mitten. The two separate parts of Michigan are stitched together by Mackinac Bridge's iron thread. Our state touches four of the five Great Lakes, only Lake Ontario is beyond our edges.

The waters that encircle the state flow through Lake Erie, then north up the Niagara River, cascading over the precipice of Niagara Falls. The waters then rest in Lake Ontario a bit before slipping out the St. Lawrence River to the Atlantic Ocean.

Did you know that every drop of water in the Great Lakes is heading toward the Atlantic? A drop of rain that falls into the southernmost corner of Lake Michigan near Chicago or that flows in past the northwestern city of Duluth into Lake Superior will take hundreds of years to move through the Great Lakes system before finally reaching the sea. Think about it. Some of the water cascading over Niagara Falls at this moment may have been in Lake Superior when French Voyageurs paddled their canoes to trade with the Native Americans and gather the pelts of animals.

These waters are on a slow, persistent journey.

And soon, again, I would join them on a long journey of my own.


## Untethered

As a backdrop to this new undertaking, in the fall of 2011, there was a seismic shift in my personal life: my husband and I split. It was not born out of my sudden empowerment or headstrong ways. It had been the plan for many years. We had stayed together for the kids. And now with both boys in college, it was time to separate, pull apart, sever the ties between us.

This was hard, but not as hard as the staying together had been. At least for me. Jim wanted to remain a couple, to keep society from unraveling, to be an example for our boys. I had already been that example, though, providing a loving home for Ben and Lucas even while the love eroded within the marriage.

So it was with a sense that a timer had gone off, that I – in the gentlest way I could – left the marriage. I packed away my books and things and put them in a tiny 8x10 storage unit, placing only the essentials in my car. And I moved for a time to the lake, my lake, Lake Michigan, to a rented house near South Haven, then one in Harbert for the remainder of the year. After unloading my things at the first house, I stretched out on a daybed on the porch in a pool of sunshine. With the waves murmuring in the distance, I drifted into an easy, light sleep, still aware of the warmth of the sunshine and the lake breeze moving over me. I felt at peace for the first time in years.

Soon, I began to type the first draft of this introduction at the lake house. In any pause, when I glanced up, I was looking out a wall of windows onto the water. Today, as I type these words, the lake is calm and blue-green, stretching to the horizon where there it is defined by a line of darker blue where it meets the sky. This lake is so wide – as I well know from encircling it with my steps – that at each point along that beach, the lake is not defined by land on the far side, but by only more water. Walking the perimeter of Lake Michigan has little in common with walking around a small lake; it is truly a journey on the endless arc of an inland sea.

When I told my cousin, Milene, about my plan to scale back, store my things and to be nomadic for a time, "to live unencumbered by possessions, to be homeless for a bit. I want to explore this," I told her. She replied, laughing, "Wow! You're living the dream!"

But I was. No mortgage, my car was paid off, no bills to speak of other than monthly expenses. I could move where I wanted for the next six months before embarking on another adventure, another 1,000-mile hike. This time I would touch all five Great Lakes and write this book exploring these vast and interconnected inland seas.

October in the yellow cottage began gently with weather so warm it felt like summer. There was a stretch of sunny days in the mid-seventies – with a few pushing up against eighty – that welcomed me to the lakeshore. On the warmest day, a Sunday, families flocked to the beach in their swimsuits. Most sat in beach chairs in the weakening fall sunshine, but a few waded in the water or floated on rafts or stood atop paddleboards. The bravest swam in the chilly waters.

That Sunday I took a long walk up the beach, then turned and walked back. I was sweaty by the time I reached the 64 steps that scaled the hillside back to the yellow cottage. I had lost some of the stamina gained during my 2009 circular hike. But, after only a week of walking the shoreline, I felt my hiking legs return. I could again match my stride to the pulsing of the waves. I felt my posture improve and my tummy retighten a bit. The uncertainty of walking on sand quickly tones the body. What I could not get used to as I trained was the turning back to retrace my steps to the cottage. On my first adventure, I had always hiked forward, never doubling back, never placing my boots on the same stretch of sand again.

After spending time on the shores of Lake Michigan, I headed to my sister's vacation home in North Carolina in the New Year to continue training for the hike and to delve further into scientific papers and books, historical documents, and first-person accounts describing the Great Lakes. My newfound mobility, moving several times in several months, encouraged me to winnow my possessions to what was necessary in order to continue my work and writing. What was necessary to hold onto? Much of what I owned had already been scrutinized and sorted to determine if it was worthy of storage during this transitional phase. Goodwill benefitted greatly as I cast off the unnecessary. I had left our family house as intact as possible so when my sons returned there on breaks it would not seem too vacant or stripped of furniture they had grown accustom to. I packed up my home office, though, the one room that was completely mine.

But then, with a mid-size car to get me from place-to-next-place, I had to determine if any item – an extra pillow, my favorite skillet, an extra pair of hiking socks – was worthy of space in my car. The winnowing process became increasingly pragmatic as I moved four times in four months. I was able to strip down to a few boxes of possessions and clothes, my computer and printer, a box of books, and a framed photo of my sons. While my car was stuffed to the roof for the first move, the backseat was mostly empty and nothing was in the passenger seat up front for the move south. This casting off contributed to the feeling of the snapping of ties to people and places and even to the earth.

In many ways it was incredibly freeing, this vagabond phase. And in other ways it was terrifying and isolating in a way I had not anticipated. I had usually been happy to be alone, solitary, working and reading and writing, but these life changes and serial migrations shook me. It was during the time in North Carolina that I finally re-centered myself in my new life. I threw myself into training and into my work and found myself all over again. I had short stories and a novel to revise, and a tall stack of books to read to research for this adventure.

Reading and writing and training filled my days from morning to late night. Hiking and running on the ocean beach, I would stop to look at a rare shell or a washed-up jellyfish. I often matched my stride to the progress of dolphins feeding offshore, parallel to where I was jogging. Afternoons were filled with reading and writing, and it was in the writing, especially, that I found myself by finding my voice and characters and stories.

Many women stay in routines and relationships because they fear change and fear being alone. I had stripped my life and possessions to the bare minimum and had found myself again. And when I was strong in myself, I strengthened the good relationships I had and sought new connections that would enrich my evolving life. And I pushed my body in my training sessions, breaking a sweat, going farther each week, pushing through the pain to get stronger in preparation for this 1,000-mile hike. Even at 48 years old, I was able to retrain my body and focus my mind on the adventure ahead.

## A 1,000-Mile Great Lakes Walk

I found a satellite image of the Great Lakes, one taken on a rare, cloudless day. The land is verdant and lush with trees. Wide rivers snake through the region as they drain the land and merge with the lakes. Large cities are visible from space; their concrete slabs erasing the green. This became the background on my computer screen, and daily I studied it consciously, while my unconscious began to absorb it in another way. This image fed the conception of this next adventure: a hike that would touch the shores of all five lakes.

This journey could have taken many different paths. It might have made sense to measure out 200-mile portions on all five lakes and walk those as five segments. I considered this, but during my first hike I became fascinated with Michigan's connection to the lakes, so I planned to do much of this adventure along that state's watery edge. Perhaps it was a personal homing instinct, but I also felt like Michigan was a sort of metaphorical base for the entire Great Lakes system as well. Each state or province in the region relates to the lakes, but Michigan connects to most of them. While it may not be the beginning or the end, perhaps it is the center.

I also wanted to explore how the lakes worked as a system, how they flow on their way to the sea. So I decided to begin in Ohio and then walk all of Michigan's Lower Peninsula's eastern edge in order to touch Lakes Erie and Huron. Walking this edge would also take me along the length of the Detroit River, Lake Saint Clair, and the Saint Clair River. These waterways connect Lakes Huron and Erie. This is the most complex connection within the Great Lakes system.

Some may wonder why I hiked along Lake Michigan at all since I had completely encircled it on my first adventure. This was purely a personal quest to retrace my steps along some of the most exquisite bits of lake beach found anywhere in the world. Plus, I had caught some grief from people for cutting across the middle of the Leelanau Peninsula instead of hiking to the tip past the lovely town of Northport. I was eager to make amends. I love this piece of Michigan – the pinky, if you will – and wanted to explore it this time and maybe even get out to the Manitou Islands. And I wanted to explore the Sleeping Bear Dunes National Lakeshore at a more leisurely pace.

After walking those routes, I would jump up to the north. Lake Superior is the wildest of the lakes, the biggest and deepest. It contains more water than the other four lakes *combined*. This greatest of lakes was shaped by massive ice sheets grinding down from the north, but it was also shaped by volcanic and tectonic forces long before the onslaught of the mountains of ice. Some of the stones along the shoreline are unique because of this. You can find agates up there, strange, translucent stones formed by water dripping through voids in the cooled lava. The water slowly deposits minerals into these voids and the minerals accumulate into pebbles, then stones over hundreds of thousands of years. When polished, agates may look like clear, glass marbles or may have layers of color inside like the most ornate, natural jewel.

There are many places along the shore of Superior where primordial forests or tall cliffs skirt the lake making it nearly impossible to walk the water's edge. I didn't want to thrash through a forest, so I chose two accessible and gorgeous stretches along Superior to explore: Pictured Rock National Lakeshore and the edge of the Keweenaw Peninsula up near Copper Harbor.

To get to the fifth lake, Lake Ontario, I would have to travel a long way. Canada borders four Great Lakes (Lake Michigan is the only one completely within America's borders), so I decided to hike along Lake Ontario on the Canadian side to explore how our neighbors to the north connect and commune with these inland seas. The largest city on the shores of Lake Ontario is Toronto, so I decided to begin in Belleville and hike west to Toronto along the lake's northern shore. The eastern curve of Lake Ontario has large bay-mouth sand dunes, and many of those formations have been protected on both the Ontario and New York side of the lake. I had never seen these dunes, so I also planned to do a day hike at the Sandbanks Provincial Park to explore them a bit.

For the finale of this hike, I chose the place to most dramatically visualize how these fresh waters move. The water that cascades over the escarpment at Niagara Falls comes from the lakes before it — Superior, Michigan, Huron, and Erie — and flows over the falls and up the Niagara River to Lake Ontario before gliding up the St. Lawrence River past Montreal and Quebec, then slipping into the Gulf of St. Lawrence, easing past Newfoundland, and finally merging with the North Atlantic.

I would end this adventure where the waters take their plunge at Niagara; the Horseshoe Falls would be my finish line.

And so a journey of 1,000 miles was assembled from these parts.

## Our vast inland seas

Think about every body of fresh water you've seen in North America outside the Great Lakes. Every creek, stream and river, flowing to a pond or lake. Maybe you've seen some of the other large lakes in America: Crater Lake or Lake Tahoe. Maybe you've watched the mighty Mississippi flowing southward on its great journey or seen the convergence of the three rivers in Pittsburgh or canoed the wilderness Boundary Waters in Minnesota. Or maybe you've seen Lake Winnipeg or Great Bear Lake in Canada. If you could gather every drop from all non-Great Lake sources, you would hold only sixteen percent of the fresh, surface water on the North American continent. This is because the Great Lakes contain the other eighty-four percent.

Pause with me for a moment to more fully grasp that. The five Great Lakes contain eighty-four percent — almost all — of North America's fresh, surface water.

When the topic of the Great Lakes comes up with people who love the lakes, they are often frustrated at how underappreciated and little known they are to people who have never seen them. I've heard accounts of people bringing friends from the coasts to the lakeshore. These visitors are often dubious about going to the lake, but then are astonished when they stand with their toes in the sand looking out onto the surface of the water that stretches unbroken to the horizon. They marvel at the wave action, the clarity of the water, the limestone or sandstone or clay cliffs, the soaring sand dunes. On windy days, they might catch sight of a kite boarder, those maniacs who strap themselves to an arc of silk that fills with wind and hurls them atop waves on the small board they've strapped to their feet. On especially wild days on the lakes, they might even see a surfer catch a curling wave. We enjoy taking these visitors to places where they can see a lake freighter, maybe a toy-sized ship balancing on the horizon, or even passing by within a stone's throw on one of the rivers these massive ships move through – like a sky scraper on its side – the people working on the ship now miniature as the ship's immensity shrinks them.

It is my hope that this book will bring a greater understanding of the Great Lakes and draw more people to their shores. And I hope that understanding evolves into appreciation and a connection to these waters . . . and that, in turn, compels people to protect and conserve this natural wonder, our Great Lakes.

Here, I will stitch together the stories of the lakes, take you with me along their shores, and explore the unique geology and personality of each Great Lake.

And so much more will happen along the way.

Walk with me once again. . . .

# *April*

**Port Clinton (and South Bass Island), Ohio, to Bay City, Michigan;
Lake Erie to Detroit River to Lake St. Clair
to St. Clair River to Lake Huron**

**302 miles in 23 days**

## Begin at the beginning

This hike would be done in segments, like my last adventure, but this time the segments would be bigger and the pace more leisurely. My hike around Lake Michigan took 64 days and averaged 16 miles a day. Whew! I had pushed myself to be able to fit the 1,000-mile hike into my life with kids still at home. This time I had more time. I planned a pace that would allow me to meet with more experts along the way, to spend more time visiting interesting sites on my route, and to even take a rest day off within the larger segments. For this type of hiking, I would use my biggest backpack.

I should probably take a moment to acquaint you with the backpack I was to become thoroughly acquainted with on this adventure. I had barely broken it in on my first hike, carrying it only on two parts of the hike where I did some camping. With this journey, it would be with me the entire way.

Modern backpacks are designed differently for women, allowing us to settle more weight on our hips than on our shoulders. This backpack was the first one I had ever owned that was designed this way. What possessed me to choose one that was white (with gray sides), I can't remember; I suspect it was on sale. They no longer make this model, and I've never seen another white one on the back of another hiker or in stores. It is large enough to allow me to pack all my camping gear when I needed it, along with food, a mini-stove, rain gear, clothing, my journal, and my iPad. I would use the iPad for my navigation and to keep in touch with friends and family.

The very first chunk of my journey would take me from the city of Port Clinton, Ohio, on the shores of Lake Erie, through Toledo where the muddy Maumee River spills into Lake Erie. From there, I'd follow the outer edge of Michigan's "thumb" all the way to Bay City. This 302-mile hike would allow me to touch Lake Erie, Lake Huron, and the waterways that connect them. It would also take me past two magnificent bridges connecting the state of Michigan to Canada: the Ambassador Bridge in Detroit, and the Blue Water Bridge in Port Huron.

Hiking alongside the Detroit River would take me through the most industrialized part of my journey. My family has three generations of ties to the Ford Motor Company, and my hike would allow me to see Henry Ford's ore-to-auto vision come alive at the River Rouge plant. I have taken a tour of this facility, walked the elevated loop around the plant and watched a naked truck frame get fitted with engine, seats, cab, doors, dash, bed, glass, and thousands of other pieces in an elegant, industrial ballet. At the end of the line, the engine is fired up and the brand-new truck is driven away.

This portion of the hike would also allow me to fully explore Michigan's "thumb." The city of Port Huron holds rich history at the place where Lake Huron flows into the St. Clair River. Just across that river in Sarnia, Ontario, is where oil in North America was first brought up from the earth by drilling. The "thumb" is mostly agrarian, its lakeshore rocky. Chemical companies bloomed in the crook of the "thumb" due to rich, natural, briny pockets in the sandstone bedrock left behind from ancient, salty seas. In places the brines are six-times more salty than the oceans. Herbert Henry Dow founded his chemical company here in the city of Midland. He began his work in an old converted flourmill, pumping liquids from the earth and developing methods to extract pure bromine and chlorine from the prehistoric brine.

## The youngest Great Lake

I drove to my sister Leslie's house and left my car there. Leslie then drove us to pick up Milene, our cousin. Together, they were going to make a day of driving me to the beginning point of my adventure. This was a festive beginning, and I thought back to my first hike where I took a train into Chicago alone to begin my hike along Lake Michigan's southern edge. While my first hike began in solitude, this one began with two of my favorite people.

After a wonderful brunch at a winery near Port Clinton, we visited the Marblehead Lighthouse. This squat, stone tower is the oldest one on the shores of the Great Lakes, and I wanted to see it sitting at the entry to Sandusky Bay. The three of us had been through the area many times to visit our Cleveland cousins. We had even waterskied on the bay here. Our more competent waterskiing cousins, the Klenkar family, would rate our wipeouts by how many times we twirled in the air before splashing into the water, or how far our skis had flung from the place we bobbed after each spill. They were continually impressed with our incompetence.

The day was gray and foggy, and we could barely make out Cedar Point, that huge amusement park, across the water from the lighthouse. There was just a ghost of tangled roller coaster tracks in the mist. It was a chatty, festive beginning to a month I would walk alone with just my strange, white backpack for company. Les and Milene even managed to find a few open shops to dash through before I began my hike that day. If you read my first book, you'll remember that they are shoppers, not hikers. They gave me a cheerful send-off, then they drove back home, and I began my journey along the shores of Lake Erie alone.

By water volume, Lake Erie is the smallest of the Great Lakes, the runt of the group. It is also the youngest. After the ice sheets retreated (about 10,000 years ago), the upper lakes (Michigan, Huron and Superior) drained to the north for a time, then flowed directly into Lake Ontario as the northern lands rebounded from being depressed by the weight of the ice. It has only been in the last 5,000 years or so that the lakes have flowed in the manner they flow today: the water from the upper lakes flowing into Erie, then Erie flowing north to Lake Ontario.

Its shallowness and orientation make Lake Erie more of a threat to boaters than you might expect given its diminutive size. When storms push over the lake from the west, this littlest of the Great Lakes can quickly transform into a raging monster.

Exactly 200 years before my hike, the winds of war blew on this lake during the second war between the British and Americans.

## The Battle of Lake Erie

The War of 1812 is often glossed over in history classes (as least the ones I took), but it's one of those wars that even the most casual student can accurately place in time.

Yep. It started in 1812.

Not much else stuck in my mind, I confess. But as I began to research the areas I would be hiking, the war kept popping up. The War of 1812 was a pivotal moment in American History. With help from the French, the American colonists had fought the British to gain independence about three decades prior to this conflict, but as the 19th century began, the British still held parts of Canada and they desired to expand their foothold in the New World. They had their eye on the eastern part of the Great Lakes region.

During my 2009 hike around Lake Michigan, this history had rarely come up (though Fort Dearborn in Chicago was indeed destroyed during The War of 1812), because in the early years of the 19th century, Lake Michigan was considered the wild west, and was not the site of key battles that occurred on land and water in the more eastern parts of the Great Lakes region. People actually referred to a trip to Chicago as "going west into the wilderness" in the early 1800s. Chicago – today the largest city on the shores of the Great Lakes – had only a few private homes prior to 1812.

After Fort Dearborn fell, just about everyone fled the town.

During The War of 1812, the British would also take Washington City (as Washington D.C. was then called), burning both the White House and the Capital Building. These were dark days for the new nation. Early in the war, much of the action took place on water, both along the Atlantic Seaboard and on the waterways going into the interior of the country.

There is a monument today on South Bass Island (in Lake Erie) not far offshore from the Marblehead Lighthouse in Ohio. It was from the bay there, Put-in-Bay, that Commodore Oliver Hazard Perry had sailed his squadron out to meet the British ships on Lake Erie. The monument on the island, a 352-foot tall Doric column, is so massive it is visible from the ferry dock east of Port Clinton.

One fascinating historical piece I read about Lake Erie was a first-hand account from the surgeon, Dr. Usher Parsons, who had been aboard Commodore Perry's flagship during the Battle of Lake Erie. While I was hiking along the placid shores of the lake, I found it difficult to imagine a raging naval battle, but Dr. Parsons told a harrowing tale of death and carnage during this three-hour battle that took place here between the British and the Americans 200 years ago. At one point, the surgeon had just finished splinting the arm of a wounded sailor, with his hand still upon the man, when a cannonball crashed through the wall of the ship, the *Lawrence,* obliterating the sailor inches away from the surgeon. It was a bloody battle. Out of the 100 men on the flagship, 83 were either killed or wounded.

It was Commodore Perry's determination that won this battle. When all the cannons on his ship were disabled along with most of his crew, he took down his personal flag, got into a skiff (the only one not destroyed), and had a couple of men row him to another of the ships under his command, the *Niagara,* that had hung back from the battle and was undamaged. Perry flew his flag and took command of the vessel and ordered it into the fray. Within minutes, the new rounds of broadsides from the fresh ship turned the tide, finishing off the weakened British ships.

The Doctor's account of the surrender of the British officers to Commodore Perry witnessed how when the British tried to hand over their swords, Perry declined and let the officers keep them. Perry offered help to their wounded and wished for the British Commander's recovery. While the dead sailors were buried at sea, the dead officers were taken ashore and

British and Americans were intermixed for burial.

But the 28-year-old naval leader was not without pride in the victory; Perry was the first in history to defeat an entire British squadron and successfully bring back every ship to his base as a prize of war. Following the Battle of Lake Erie, Perry penned the famous words, "We have met the enemy and they are ours . . ." in his report to General William Henry Harrison.

Today, both British and American officers are buried underneath the Doric column monument at Put-in-Bay. While the Treaty of Ghent was signed in 1814 to end the war, another agreement was signed in 1817 that resulted in a lasting peace between the U.S. and Canada. The monument on the island is more than a monument to a naval victory. It is called the Perry Victory & International Peace Memorial because it also honors the enduring peace in the region and the longest undefended international border in the world at over 4,000 miles long. Over a quarter of this border passes through the middle of four of the Great Lakes, and almost half is a watery border if you include the length of the St. Lawrence River.

## The Walleye Capital

Port Clinton, where I began my hike, is spackled with the Perry name: Perry Street, Commodore Perry Inn and Suites, Camp Perry, Perry Pier, and so on. Camp Perry, a National Guard training facility, boasts the largest outdoor rifle range in the world. Shots are fired into a berm of dirt near the lakeshore, so I didn't attempt to walk the shoreline here. There is also a storage facility for army ordinance (missiles and bombs). I kept to the road to be safe and remain in one piece, a wise decision considering it was just the beginning of my long walk and I would make quite a target carrying my bright white backpack.

Port Clinton is the Walleye Capital of the World, I learned. This fish is a prized catch. They can grow to over 2 feet long and weigh over 20 pounds, and they are delicious.

"It is also the mayfly capital!" Deb, the owner of the Touch of Italy B&B in Port Clinton told me.

The mayfly is a harmless, winged insect (the most prolific in Lake Erie being of the genus *Hexagenia)* that tends to hatch synchronously and in such large numbers that dense clouds of them can be tracked on Doppler radar. From its head to the end of its abdomen, this species of mayfly is about an inch long, but long "tails" in back and extra-long front legs that they hold out in front of them double this size.

In Port Clinton in the spring, they have to use the city's snowplows to clear the streets of millions of these dead insects so cars don't slide around on roads slick with squashed bugs.

"They even turn the street lights off at night so the bugs aren't drawn inland," Deb told me. "One night they didn't turn off the light where my husband had parked his car and in the morning it was covered with three inches of dead mayflies."

That's the other problem: not only do they synchronize their hatching, they also die at the same time because they only live for three days as adults. During this time, they are focused on mating and laying fresh eggs in the lake.

Although this sounds like an insect invasion (and it is), it has a silver lining. Lake Erie was purged of mayflies for decades due to heavy pollution, so their return is a good indication that the lake is recovering. I was happy to learn about the brief, annual cloud of mayflies without having to walk through it. Most of the year, locals and visitors can focus on the tasty walleye that the city is better known for.

## Black swamp and long flights

The southwestern shore of Lake Erie, today, is quite marshy. When Americans were trying to settle to the west, migrating into Michigan and Indiana in the late 18th and early 19th century, they were confronted by the dense, primeval swamp that stretched from where Sandusky, Ohio, is today all the way to Fort Wayne, Indiana. And it wasn't a thin stretch of swamp. It was forty miles wide for most of that way, created by glacial moraines keeping water in the area and a dense deposit of clay that prevented the water from seeping into the ground. Settlers called it "The Great Black Swamp." They dreaded getting lost in it or contracting one of the many "fever diseases" people came down with after getting eaten alive by the swarming clouds of gnats and flies there. Even Native Americans avoided this area except to hunt, and they only did that by staying on the sandy ridges left by the retreating glaciers.

The thick, deep mud there was known to be able to swallow wagons whole. Travelers on horseback that entered the area would return – if they were lucky – with their horses and themselves welted, running with blood from wounds where biting flies had taken chunks of their flesh. It was common for people to enter the swamp and never emerge.

When they finally built a road through the horrible place in the 1820s, inns sprang up along it at intervals of just a mile between them. That's because it was a good day if travelers could make a mile a day on it. The road's nickname, Mud Pike, was well earned. Some enterprising innkeepers complicated matters by maintaining the worst of the mud holes located conveniently near their establishments to ensure that travelers would need their assistance and a place to stay the night. One innkeeper even legally transferred the title to his mud hole when he sold his inn.

When a system of canals was dredged through the swamp, a company in Montreal sent in teams of French Canadian choppers to harvest the ancient white oaks to be used for ship's timbers. They moved into the swamp in teams of around a hundred men, choosing oaks that were so large there was more than fifty feet between the ground and the first branch. They felled these giants that had once prevented sunlight from reaching the floor of the swamp, squared off the tree trunks, lashed them together with lighter logs to keep them afloat and used the canals and mules to tow the massive logs to Toledo. From there, boats took the timbers to Montreal where they were loaded onto steamships and transported across the Atlantic to the shipyards of Europe.

A large remnant – 12,000 acres – of this muddy landscape is now protected along Lake Erie's edge. The Magee Marsh portion has been tamed, the mammoth oak, hickory, elm and ash trees long removed, the water now controlled with dikes and pumps and channels. A paved road leads to a parking lot on the edge of Lake Erie, and a boardwalk winds through the swampy land nearby.

I saw hundreds of birds as I walked there: ducks and grebes, cormorants and coots, geese, egrets and herons. There were even a few songbirds singing to each other. I looked out onto the gray waters of Lake Erie for a moment, then hiked inland to the Black Swamp Bird Observatory headquarters, where I stopped in to meet with Kim Kaufman, the Executive Director. She wore a gray, hoodie sweatshirt emblazoned with the name of the place, her long dark hair falling past her shoulders.

We went to the center's multi-purpose room: part office, part conference room, part storage. I unbuckled the waist belt of my pack and shrugged it off, then leaned it and my walking pole against the wall.

"That's quite a pack," she said as I sat down with her.

"I'm using my big pack on this hike," I said. I flexed my tired shoulders. It would take a while to become comfortable with the size and weight. The white backpack would be my companion on the entire journey – a companion that weighed up to 35 pounds and always insisted on riding on my back.

"This marsh is vital to around two hundred species of birds that migrate through here," Kim told me. "When they arrive after flying from as far away as South America, they see the expanse of Lake Erie's water and drop down into the marsh to rest. The males are in full fledge, and they take a break here to feed and sing and recuperate before continuing to their destination. Some birds end up in northern Canada."

Many of the birds fly astounding distances, and these rest stations are crucial to their journeys, she noted. "In the fall, one bird, the Blackpoll Warbler, migrates through here and flies non-stop for about 80 hours from here all the way back to South America."

Kim told me about the important research done at the center, including an active banding program to help track bird migration. They have banded over a half-million birds over the years. I asked Kim about a faded U.S. map on the wall studded with colorful pushpins.

"Those pins represent where our banded birds have been recovered," she said.

I asked her about funding from the Great Lakes Restoration Initiative. This five-year government initiative was designed to support multiple efforts to conserve and restore the Great Lakes.

"Yes! We've been able to employ about twenty people with grants from that source."

"I went to a meeting before the program started," I told her, "and a recurring comment was that there should be an education component to the funding."

"That's a huge part of our work," she nodded enthusiastically. "We have school groups through here all the time and many of the kids help with the banding."

"What a great way to connect them to the birds."

"And to nature in general. It's so much more effective than a lecture or a book or even a movie. If these kids don't care about the environment, there won't be anyone to continue this work."

I thanked Kim for her time. Then I grasped the upper handle on my backpack and swung it around, looping first my left arm, then my right through the shoulder straps. I shrugged my shoulders while I cinched the waist belt, then lowered them to let most of the weight settle again on my hips. Then I grabbed my aluminum walking pole, and headed out into the sunny, windy, Ohio day.

As I hiked west toward Toledo, the roads were paralleled with deep, water-filled ditches. Pipes drained water from the fields. One of the mornings was rainy and the freshly plowed acreage blossomed with puddles that often merged into growing ponds. In one field, the water was deep enough that ten swans landed and paddled around together, visiting.

This land, I realized, still longs to return to marsh. If we cease our efforts to tame it, drain the fields and pump the water away in roadside ditches, it would again transform into The Great Black Swamp.

There isn't much beach along this stretch, but Maumee State Park just east of Toledo has tamed the swamp enough to have a small one. I hiked through the park to get to the edge of Lake Erie. The water is perpetually muddy here due to the Maumee River emptying into the lake nearby. This river begins near Fort Wayne, Indiana, and brings with it sediment and silt as it merges with the lake.

A crunching sound underneath my boots made me look down to see thousands of zebra mussel shells on the shore. These invasive mussels have been filtering the waters of the Great Lakes for decades now. In the distance across the water, I could see the enormous power plant in Monroe, Michigan.

I encountered a retired boilermaker, Nate, who lives near the State Park.

"What's the biggest boiler you've ever worked on?" I asked.

He nodded toward the north. "The plant in Monroe. It was the largest coal-fired plant in the country when it was built. The firebox is 12 stories tall. It would take carpenters two weeks just to build the scaffolding we needed to reach sections of pipe that needed to be replaced."

"So you actually work where the coal is burned?"

He nodded. "The firebox is lined with pipes that carry the water to be heated. The pipes wear out over time, and we remove those sections that are weak and put in new piping."

I asked him if he'd worked elsewhere.

"I've worked on some lake freighters. Most people don't know there is still steam power on the lakes."

"I heard that only the Badger Ferry burns coal."

"Right. These freighters burn diesel fuel #6. It's thick like molasses until heated, then it thins to a maple-syrup consistency. They atomize it into the boilers and ignite it to heat water to steam."

We chatted for a while about electricity and the future of generating power in America. Nate, a man who had spent his life scaling the interior of sooty, cavernous fireboxes, was dubious about moving away from coal to greener sources of fuel.

After walking along a dense industrial area, I crossed over the Maumee River. The city of Toledo had a nice pedestrian corridor winding through their factory district. They had recently built a modern bridge lofting over the old drawbridge. The old bridge had been partitioned, designating half of it for bicycles and pedestrians. After scurrying over many bridges and overpasses on the narrow strip between a concrete wall and streaming traffic, it was pleasant crossing the Maumee River at a more leisurely pace.

I stopped a few times on the bridge to look at the skyline of downtown Toledo, to watch the geese and ducks on the river, to study the mounds of raw materials heaped along its banks, and to just peer down into the muddy water without having to worry about becoming a decoration on the grill of a semi-truck.

## Procurer of skulls

A woman living in Southeast Michigan asked to meet up with me when I was passing near her. I hiked the overpass to get beyond I-75 and crossed a couple of low bridges spanning the inlets and large creeks flowing to merge with Lake Erie to get to our meeting place.

Sally Thompson told me she was an artist and an avid kayaker. I was pleased to be meeting up with someone who not only knew this area, but also loved it enough to do beautiful, modern paintings of it. She jumped out of her little SUV and walked out to meet me. She is a short woman in her late 40s with bright eyes and a wide smile. Her wild brown hair was escaping from a loose ponytail.

"So nice to meet you!" Sally said.

"It's my pleasure," I answered. "I see that there are a lot of inlets along here. Is this where you kayak?"

"Yes. All along this western edge of Erie. Many of the inlets bloom with lotus in the summer. It's gorgeous."

"Did you want to walk this point, or was there somewhere else you wanted to show me?"

"Jump in," she said.

I put my pack in the back seat, wedging it in so it would be safe, and climbed into the front. Sally said it was best to drive out to a couple of access points where we could see Lake Erie and walk a bit. These places were removed from the main road I otherwise needed to follow to safely circumvent lakeside obstacles in this stretch. In particular, I had e-mailed her a couple weeks prior about the best way to get around Monroe's power plant.

"I spoke to the guard at the plant," she told me. "He said that the field you wanted to cross is pretty boggy right now. I can take us to the stretch of beach by the plant, though, and we can walk there. I'll show you this area first."

We drove along a wide inlet for a while. Out in the water, there was a large, wooden platform. I couldn't quite tell what it was or what it was doing there.

"Is that part of an old barge?" I asked.

"That's a fish farm," she said. "There's a huge net underneath it filled with fish. When fishermen catch a big carp, they toss it onto that platform and the eagles come and eat it."

"Wow," I said.

"I just feel so bad for the fish in the farm," Sally said, glancing around with a worried look. "They've got to be so nervous when that happens!" We laughed together.

When we passed a cove with many piers, Sally handed me her business card. "That's my painting of this view," she said, pointing out my window. I held her card up with the reproduction of her colorful painting, matching up the piers and grasses that grew along the edge. Her technique was modern and colorful, not quite abstract expressionist, but heading that way. I thought she had brought vibrant life to the placid scene. Her love of this place came through in her art.

Sally parked in a rutted gravel lot near Monroe's massive power plant. We walked past a man loading his Labrador retriever into his truck, then through an open gate toward Lake Erie. The lake was choppy. The sunlight glinted off the surface of the water, silvering it like the top was liquid mercury. The Toledo Harbor lighthouse held its place several miles offshore on a manmade island of rock and concrete. To the southeast I could see the steam billowing from the nuclear power plant near Port Clinton.

"I walked by that plant four days ago," I told Sally.

"It must be exciting to look back along the lakeshore like that."

"It puts it into perspective," I said.

We walked along the narrow beach. It was strewn with last year's lotus pods, driftwood, and plastic debris. When we came upon a dead white egret, Sally found a forked stick and pinned its neck to the sand. "I don't have one of these," she said as she began to pull and twist the head. Since I had a bit of a fascination with road kill myself from my first long hike, I hadn't been too alarmed when she stopped to look at it, but I began to worry as she struggled to decapitate it.

"Ah . . . I have a knife in my pack in the car," I said, trying to be helpful.

"You don't see them with the heads usually," Sally said as she struggled with the extra-tough ligaments still holding the skull to the neck. "Predators usually eat them."

*Interesting point,* I thought inside my own skull.

Soon she had the bird head removed and she turned it over and around, studying it from all sides. "I have a collection of skulls that I study for my art. I sketch them to get the animal forms just right."

That made perfect sense to me.

"Hold it up," I said as I raised my camera. She held the little skull next to her head, and the beak opened in a pleasant echo of Sally's broad smile.

We walked the shore until we reached a metal barrier. It blocked the beach where the power plant expelled hot water back into the lake. A sign attached to the barrier stated: "PEOPLE DIE HERE: Several people have drowned in the swift undertow at this location. They failed to obey the warning signs. Do NOT wade or swim in this area."

I had never seen a sign with a clearer message.

"A three-year-old died here," Sally said. "I'm glad they put up a sign."

I later learned that the eagles have started to stay in the area through the winter. When ice formed elsewhere on the lake, they could continue to fish in the warmer water near the power plant that stayed perpetually open.

Sally drove me to a bridge I'd have to cross to continue my hike to the city of Monroe. I said goodbye to her, with a wave as well to her newly acquired egret skull, hoisted my backpack, and began walking north once again.

## Monroe, or as it was formerly known, Frenchtown

"Remember the Raisin" is a strange thing to yell. It seems like something you might expect to hear exclaimed in the kitchen during fruitcake season, not a battle cry that spurred soldiers to war long ago. Indeed, the Americans shouted this curious phrase during The War of 1812 to inspire memories of the massacre that took place along the shores of the River Raisin (named for the plentiful grapes that grew along the banks there).

An amazing man rose up to lead the Native Americans to war during this conflict. But Tecumseh – he was born on a night when a meteor streaked across the sky and his name means "shooting star" – was more than a great warrior. He was an orator, a thinker, a leader of men, a negotiator. He was, in short, a visionary. He moved the philosophy of his people away from a stubborn adherence to the Native concept that no one could own the land – they had certainly seen that the white men could push them from their traditional territory and claim it as their own – to the concept that the indigenous peoples had rights to the land that they had lived on for countless generations.

The Governor of Indiana, William Henry Harrison, was constantly pushing the Native Americans west. His goal was to settle enough land so Indiana could apply for statehood. He had several intense negotiations with Tecumseh and wrote this assessment of the warrior chief to the United States War Department: "[Tecumseh] is one of those uncommon geniuses which spring up occasionally to produce revolution. . . . If it were not for the vicinity of the United States he would, perhaps, be the founder of an empire that would rival in glory Mexico or Peru."

Prior to The War of 1812, Tecumseh travelled thousands of miles amongst tribes and factions to band his people into one fighting force. Then, just as he completed this monumental task, President Madison declared war on Britain. Tecumseh quickly made an alliance with the enemy of his enemy and fought alongside British forces. His goal was to restore his homeland to his people, to claim Ohio – once and for all – to be forever their land. And to gain the advantage of thousands of warriors fighting on their side, the British promised them this homeland if they won the war.

The battle along the River Raisin took place in the frigid days of January 1813. As I hiked through the city of Monroe, I noticed streets named Kentucky Avenue and Kentucky Court. This struck me as odd. I hiked to the visitor center at the battlefield, unbuckled and shrugged off my pack and leaned it with an affectionate pat against the building out of the way, and went inside. Spying a set of double doors leading to a room where a presentation was in progress, I slipped into the back of the small hall and settled in a chair. There were two maps on the wall. As a recorded narrator spoke, various lines of colored lights lit up to demonstrate troop movements and clashes.

Since the war was fought in January, the River Raisin was frozen solid and troops skittered back and forth across the slippery surface during the several days of the battle. The Americans were outnumbered by more than three to one. Knowing it was hopeless, many surrendered to the British and Native American forces. When the British marched out of town the next day, the native warriors turned on the captives and massacred most of them. In the end, only 33 of the over 900 Americans escaped this battle with their lives. Most of the Americans who fought and died here were Kentuckians who had marched north to join the fight. Tecumseh was not at this particular battle, which was unfortunate because this fierce warrior was known for his fair treatment of the wounded and captured. He most certainly would have prevented the massacre.

Tecumseh and his warriors fought bravely throughout the war and were successful when the British did their part. Without the help of British cannons, though, the Native Americans could not take forts. When the British leadership or armament faltered, Tecumseh's men couldn't carry the battle alone.

## A big island and walleyed fish

After spending the night near the city of Monroe, I continued hiking north along Lake Erie's western edge, planning to make it to the island of Grosse

Ile (French for "Big Island" and pronounced *Gross Eel)* in one day. This island sits at the southern end of the Detroit River where it flows into Lake Erie. I kept mostly to roads, due to Lake Erie's marshy edge and also the Fermi II Nuclear Power plant along the shore here.

Just before I reached the island, I hiked through Trenton. As I passed through the drab, industrialized riverfront of Trenton, with its ghastly brick power plant, and then crossed a bridge onto the verdant island of Grosse Ile, I had a flashback to the *Wizard of Oz* movie – the point where it suddenly goes from black-and-white to Technicolor.

It was a long hike, a 21-mile day, to get to the island, and I was dragging a bit and my white backpack felt heavier than usual when I finally arrived at the Pilot House Hotel at the island's south end. This building has been here for over eight decades and holds an important part of the island's history. It was the officer's quarters and club at the Naval Air Station on Grosse Ile. For many years, the Navy trained its pilots on this airfield. During WWII there were as many as 800 cadets stationed here at a time. Often they had to bunk with local residents because there were too many to house on the base. George H.W. Bush, Donald Rumsfeld, and even Bob Barker spent some of their time in the Navy on the island of Grosse Ile.

While the base closed in 1969, much of the history has been preserved. I stayed at the Pilot House Hotel for two nights and did a day hike to explore the island. As I wandered about, much lighter on my feet since I was able to leave my pack at the hotel, I discovered an alpaca farm and was invited in to visit. One does not get invited to mingle with alpaca every day. It was with fascination that I entered their enclosure and spent some pleasant time taking photos of all their silly hairdos and amusingly strange feet. Oddly enough, I felt bad that my backpack wasn't there to share the experience.

Later that day, I noticed the Detroit River was studded with fishing boats. It was walleye season.

## Captain Ken

My second evening at the Pilot House Hotel, I chatted with some of the fishermen lounging around in the common room. When they heard about the long hike I was embarking on and my interests in the lakes, one guy ran outside and brought in the captain of a charter boat.

"This is Captain Ken," he said. "He's the guy you want to talk to."

Captain Ken sat himself down in a recliner and leaned back into it, extending the footrest. I sat on the nearby couch.

"How long have you been a charter captain?" I asked.

"Twenty years. I chase mostly walleye," Captain Ken said.

"How have these waters changed over the years?"

"The water used to burn your skin if you got it on you," he said. "Like getting splashed with diesel fuel. It's much cleaner now. You can see six, eight feet down. The walleye have made a comeback now that the waters are cleaner. They are sight-feeders."

"And you feel safe eating fish out of the river here?"

"Sure," he crossed his arms.

"Really?"

"Listen," he said, leaning toward me a bit, "the way they test these fish, they put them in a blender. Whole. Then test the blended stuff. You go outside right now, you'll see my guys fileting the walleye. We take that nice filet off each side, get rid of any belly fat, and toss the rest. That's what they should be testing, just that filet."

"I think they are looking to measure overall contamination of the rivers and lakes when they do that," I offered. "The toxic burden the fish carry."

Captain Ken looked dubious.

"Do you fish in all the lakes?" I asked.

"Yep. Not Superior all that much, but all the others." He told me he owned the 21-foot boat parked in back of the hotel.

"Which lake is the most dangerous?"

"Erie. Hands down," he said. He launched right into a story, one he had clearly told many times before.

"I'm doing a charter on Erie with two guys. The lake is glass and we've almost caught our limit. The wind begins, and there is an immediate chop on the lake, and some clouds are collecting, so I tell the guys to stow the gear and we'll head in since we've caught our fish.

"The lake has one-footers by the time the gear is away – and three-footers in minutes as we head toward land. In under ten minutes, there are eight-footers.

"Eight-footers!" Captain Ken laughs, as though the memory was unnerving, even from the safety of a recliner in a hotel common room. He looks at me to see if I am impressed. My wide eyes confirm that indeed I am. He continues:

"I have to play each wave perfectly as I head toward the river, or we'll be swamped or flipped. And every wave is different because . . . well, it's Lake Erie. It takes about fifteen minutes to get to the mouth of the river, and the very last wave is a monster. I figure if I play it just right and feather it out at the end, we'll flow right into the river. If I'm off a few inches, we'll flip and be crushed on the rocks.

"And it's perfect, just perfect, and we glide into the river. I can't believe it and I look down and my white-knuckled hands won't let go of the wheel and it takes me some time to unclench my hands. When I finally turn around to look at the guys . . ." he leaned toward me ". . . one is napping and the other is pouring a cup of coffee!"

I laughed. "They had confidence in you!"

"I asked them what in the hell they were doing and they said, 'Oh, we knew you had it.' And I said, 'No . . . no . . . oh, no.' They had no idea how close we came!"


## That's the pep talk?

Since I had hiked a loop around the southern half of the island, I asked the owner of the hotel, Jim, if he would give me a lift over the bridge at the north end so I wouldn't have to cover the same ground twice. I wrestled my white backpack and my aluminum walking pole between my feet in his small car and we took off.

"Did you walk out to the Olds Mansion yesterday?" he asked.

I shook my head.

"We'll swing by there. You should see it." The Olds family (of the Oldsmobile car company) built their mansion on Elba Island that hugs the southern edge of Grosse Ile. We swung by. "These two houses . . . they were for their maid and gardener," Jim told me, pointing at two enormous homes. "That big white mansion is the main house. They still use it for fundraisers. It's gorgeous inside."

We drove on, zipping up the east side of the island, following around the northern tip, and then crossed the bridge to the mainland.

"You can drop me anywhere along here," I said.

"Where are you walking to today?" he asked.

"To Detroit. All the way downtown."

"Which way?"

"I'll stay close to the river. Take Biddle until it turns into Jefferson. Take that to the bridge, then cut over to Fort Street."

"You're walking Jefferson? That's a war zone!" Jim said, then recounted an unpleasant experience he recently had on Jefferson.

"I used to live in Detroit," I offered. "And it's Easter Sunday, so I think the war zone will be pretty deserted. But thanks for the pep talk!"

Jim pulled over at a park on the south side of Wyandotte, and I thanked him as I shouldered my pack, glad to have its weight settled on my back, its ever-present company along this stretch of the hike.

"Be careful," he called to me. "Call me if you need a ride out of there."

I made my way to the downtown of Wyandotte – a city about a dozen miles south of the center of Detroit – and headed to the riverwalk there. The day was windy and mild, sunlight streamed through gaps in the clouds. The Detroit River was green-blue, and fishermen were already out on its surface, trying to lure walleye to come home for Easter dinner. I hiked through the riverfront park and up to a fence. A mound of coal rose up on the other side.

Beyond the coal was a massive power plant. This is the first time I'd seen a power plant without the requisite buffer zone around it. All of the power plants I had passed on the shores of Lake Michigan had a large, overgrown fenced-off area that I had to skirt. Here, in Wyandotte, kids could play on swings and a slide within feet of a mound of coal. I walked around the power plant, then past the enormous complex that the BASF Corporation has along the river. The company produces a variety of urethane and specialty plastic products for various industries. BASF is Wyandotte's largest employer, and by most accounts a good partner for the conservation and cleanup efforts that have been underway for the Detroit River.

There was a short stretch along Biddle Avenue where I could see the river, then Biddle became West Jefferson Avenue and I continued north into the city of Ecorse. The riverfront here is heavily industrialized with an enormous steel mill. There were also indications that I was entering a rougher neighborhood – shattered glass on a bus shelter, burned and abandoned houses, and even a boarded-up McDonalds.

When the McDonalds shuts down, it's a rough neighborhood.

Usually I would be very in tune with these signs. On this day, though, I had a tooth that had gone from being sensitive to aching, and on to throbbing, and that was occupying my mind. I decided at the point the pain started pulsating that I needed to find a drugstore to get some toothpaste for sensitive teeth (this usually fixed the problem), but after the boarded-up McDonalds, I thought I might be out of luck. Miraculously, I found an open drugstore not too much farther. I crossed the wide road and made my way through the parking lot. I was converging at the door a little ahead of a young guy who gave me a pretty hard look, so I made sure I entered the store ahead of him and held the door open behind me for him. The hard look fell off his face and he thanked me.

After getting my toothpaste and taking a couple of painkillers, I continued through the town of River Rouge. It is here that Henry Ford's "ore-to-auto" vision came alive. Iron ore was transported across the lakes and brought in on the Detroit River on ships, while coal arrived by rail. The massive smelting furnaces were powered by the coal and turned the rock ore into molten iron. They poured the liquid metal into forms for engine blocks or onto huge, flat surfaces to roll out in large sheets. The sheets were pressed into the fenders and hoods and doors. All the parts were then gathered and assembled right there on site to make a complete vehicle.

Currently, they still assemble trucks there. The Rouge River complex includes more than twenty miles of road, at least five times that of rail, and more than a mile of boat docks.

My grandfather worked here for decades. Many summers when I was a kid, Leslie and Milene and I would have a week where we would stay with our grandparents. If my grandma wanted the car to take us somewhere in the evening, we'd have to drop my grandpa off for his afternoon shift at the Rouge. I remember my grandma packing his lunch pail with a hearty sandwich and snacks. She'd then fill his green thermos with iced tea that my grandpa brewed and sweetened himself.

I remember being fascinated by how the thermos fit perfectly into the rounded top of the lunch pail and was held in place by a wire bracket. The top was secured to the bottom with locking wire clasps that I loved to fasten and unfasten just to see how they worked.

We girls would pile into the back seat of the car for the ride down to the Rouge. My grandpa would hop out and wave goodbye, then merge with the rush of men entering the plant as the men from the day shift streamed out. My grandma would drive us out of there, past the power plant and the sparks and the industrial smells, and we'd go off to dinner and a movie together before collecting my grandpa from the plant at midnight.

At night, the darkness would mute the sounds and sights of the plant, but never the smells. Now, while hiking through the area decades later, I detected that same smell, and it brought me back to those warm, drowsy, summer nights waiting for my grandpa to emerge from the hulking factory and climb into the car to drive us home. The smell of the place clung to his work clothes, reminding us of the Rouge long after we had made it back to their home in Dearborn.

On the Sunday I hiked through the city, there was a train delivering rolls of steel to the factory. I slowed my pace when I saw the railcars streaming across the sidewalk a couple of blocks ahead. I'd have to wait for it to pass, so I took my time approaching. As I got nearer, I was surprised to see two people waiting on the other side of the train. I caught brief glimpses of them over the train car couplings, quick flashes like individual frames in a movie. These accumulated into a complete picture: two young guys, probably in their mid-teens, and they were passing something back and forth and bringing it to their lips, a joint. They hadn't noticed me – and I'm sure it never crossed their minds that a middle-aged woman would be hiking through the area on Easter – so as the final train cars neared, I had plenty of time to think about how to greet them when we suddenly came face to face when the last train car passed.

Let's face it. Waiting for a long train to pass, you have time to think. To even plot a bit.

When the last car slid by, they began walking across the tracks with their eyes down. I waited a moment, then held my arms wide and bellowed "Happy Easter!" They stopped on the tracks and looked up at me with their bloodshot eyes and dropped jaws. To freak them out, I almost added "Merry Christmas!" . . . but figured I didn't want to do permanent damage to their psyches. I chuckled as they stared at me, then at each other, then back at me, a strange single woman walking through one of America's densest industrial corridors with a white backpack on my back.

I gave a wave as I passed them and continued walking, briskly, toward Detroit.

## Rivers afire

There are four rivers within the Great Lakes basin that have caught fire. Yes, you read that correctly, these rivers have burst into flames. The most recent (and therefore the one people think of first) is the Cuyahoga River in Cleveland. It had a spectacular fire in 1969, enabled by a thick oil slick and woody brush and debris that had been gathering along the pilings of bridges. This fire became the "poster child" of the growing environmental movement; it was one of the main trigger points for passing the Clean Water Act in 1972. Flames peaked as high as fifty feet over the river before the fire was brought under control.

Unfortunately, this was not the first time that river had ignited. It had been bursting into flames periodically since 1868, with its most damaging fire in 1952. The other rivers to catch fire are the Chicago River, the Buffalo River, and the Rouge River that feeds into the Detroit River. The Rouge has so much industry along its banks that when 250,000 gallons of oil were spilled there a decade ago, investigators had to scrutinize dozens of factories and facilities that could have been responsible.

There have been multiple oil spills on the Rouge River. In 1948, a spill killed off thousands of waterfowl. Sportsmen who had hunted there for generations were so incensed that they launched their skiffs into the black, slick water, gathered all the slimy carcasses, tossed the dead and dripping ducks and geese into the back of their trucks, and drove them to Lansing. There, they lined the sidewalks of the capital. Michigan's legislators had to walk past the thousands of oil-soaked carcasses to get to their offices.

When I saw black and white photos from this time, it drove home the idea that avid hunters are also passionate about protecting the environment. Sure, hunters wanted to kill a few of those birds themselves, but they got pretty upset when they saw the wholesale killing caused by that spill. They know there would be fewer birds to return to the area in subsequent years because of such reckless actions by industry.

On my last hike, I had seen duck blinds in nature preserves, but it took me a while to make sense of the bigger picture. Hunters think about the next hunting season, or the seasons after that, when they would teach their young kids and grandkids to hunt the offspring of the birds flying overhead today.

## A wildlife refuge amongst industry

Much of the area I had hiked through north of Toledo and up to Detroit has been designated as an "International Wildlife Refuge." It may seem counter-intuitive to have a refuge in an urban area, but to the manager of the refuge, John Hartig, it makes perfect sense. This location puts it within a 45-minute drive of nearly 7 million people. The refuge includes almost 6,000 acres of shoreline, wetlands, islands and shoals, and will continue to expand as funds allow.

"Funds from the GLRI have helped to restore habitats at the Refuge Gateway, to purchase Sugar Island, and to restore Ford Marsh Unit in Monroe," Hartig told me. He explained that the challenges of managing a wildlife refuge in one of the most industrialized corridors in the Great Lakes are different from those in a more wild and remote site. "Human impact is greater here, stakeholder involvement more challenging, and transactional costs are higher," he said.

More than 100 acres were reclaimed brownfield zones. Over 200 organizations have cooperated with the conservation of the area.

"The Detroit River and western Lake Erie are quietly undergoing one of the most remarkable ecological recoveries in North America," Hartig said.

While walking, it was difficult to see the extent of the restoration, but I knew there were large stretches of wild tucked in between industry. I wished I had time to kayak the area, to see the river side of the preserve, to watch blue heron and egret spearing fish and frogs in the wetlands, to maybe even see a sturgeon, that ancient, armored fish, slip underneath the kayak and into the murky depths of the river.

Instead, I hiked with my white backpack through the city of River Rouge, past Zug Island with its pulsing steel mill and mountains of coal. I passed by Detroit's wastewater-treatment plant – the largest single-site facility of its kind in America. I smelled the plant long before I reached it, since the wind was blowing hard from the north. The smell intensified as I drew near. When I was within sight of the plant, my eyes watered from the odor, and I thought I was going to gag. Some of these facilities now dry and burn a concoction of processed waste to generate power to run their own operations. I didn't know if this took place in Detroit, but – *Holy stench, Batman!* – it smelled horrible. I walked faster to get upwind of the facility.

North of the almost visible smell, I entered the Delray area of south Detroit. It is here that the "war zone" label most aptly fit, though it was deserted. There were areas strewn with the rubble of whatever building used to stand there, and the rubble was nearly swallowed in aggressive weeds. The sidewalk and road were cracked as if they had suffered hundreds of mini-earthquakes. Plants sprouted wherever a gap opened in the pavement.

Gangs had tagged every surface, but even these declarations claiming the streets were faded and flaking, their ownership relinquished since there was no longer anything of value to claim. I could have walked down the middle of the street for blocks, letting the wind blow seeds and trash around me, as no vehicles passed by.

As I looked around, I thought they could film a post-apocalyptic movie here. As I pressed farther into the middle of the deserted zone, I thought they may have to tidy it up a bit for the movie.

I saw only one person in this stretch toward the edge of Delray. He was a shambling, homeless man dressed in rags walking on the other side of the street. I kept an eye on him, and when he saw me, he stopped. I kept walking at the same quick pace, but nodded to him. He lifted a hand and shouted, "Happy Easter!"

I chuckled and returned the greeting.

Well-played, homeless guy.


## Forts and fights and bridges

The only battle that Tecumseh and the British commander, Isaac Brock, ever fought together during The War of 1812 was in Detroit. Tecumseh had been hoping for a British commander who shared his level of intellect and resolve to fight and win this war. He found it in Brock. There was much mutual admiration between them. It is said that Brock unwound the brightly colored sash from his waist and presented it to Tecumseh as a token of his esteem.

A plan to take Fort Detroit was hatched between them. After Brock softened the American's resolve by shelling it from the Canadian side of the Detroit River, the native warriors would flood the settlement outside the fort and secure it. They were to occupy it without bloodshed if possible, fighting only if attacked. Brock would then move his lines across the river to within sight of the fort, fire some light artillery, and tell the American

General Hull that the warriors could not be held back too much longer.

General Hull was a bit of a coward and had been drinking all night in anticipation of the imminent attack. He gave up the fort without Brock and Tecumseh having to act on their threats.

After The War of 1812, the battered nation of America decided to fortify itself against future attacks and built a series of forts along its waterways. Fort Wayne was one of these installations, located along the Detroit River in a location now almost in the shadow of the Ambassador Bridge. I was looking forward to taking a break there, to seeing some green grass after walking through the war zone.

As I approached the boundary of the fort, a tall, chain-link fence topped with barbed wire kept me from accessing the fort's land. Not too far after the fence began, however, a section of it had been plowed down by an out-of-control vehicle. The fence lay strewn about, the barbed wire broken and coiling onto itself, the support posts bent in places and broken at the point of impact. I could have walked over and through this felled fence, but decided that I'd better go to the main entrance. If they were keeping people off the grounds with fencing and barbed wire, then they were probably monitoring the area for trespassers. I walked in the main entrance for cars, and a large security guard immediately stepped halfway out of the guard booth and held out his hand to stop me.

I stopped and waved. "Hi. I'm hiking all the Great Lakes this year." My voice was hoarse from the dry wind and all the dust and detritus I had been breathing, and the wind swept my words away.

"What?" The guard said warily, now mostly back inside the booth, looking afraid like I was going to pull a gun on him or do something crazy.

"Hi," I tried again, waving my red, aluminum hiking pole in the air, then turning to the side to show him my backpack. "I'm a hiker. I'm hiking through here."

He stepped all the way out of the booth and stared at me, hands on his hips, keeping an eye on my hiking pole like it was a weapon.

I lowered it slowly and stepped closer, pulling out and offering my card with a map of the Great Lakes sections I was hiking.

"You don't get many hikers?" I laughed.

"You'd be the first," he said, studying my card.

"I read about the fort and wanted to take a quick look."

"I can't allow that," he said. "We're not open yet."

"Can I just walk to the river and back?"

"Can't allow that. Technically, this is still an active military base, so we have tight access rules."

"Active?" I looked at the deserted buildings. Many had holes in the roof or boarded-up windows.

"Technically. Come back when we're open."

"I'm hiking the rest of the month, so maybe I'll make it back later in the year."

I regretted not having strolled onto the grounds when I'd passed the broken fence. Sure, they may have run me off, but I would have walked around the fort a bit. I had to be satisfied with what I could see of Fort Wayne through the fence.

I made my way toward the Ambassador Bridge. As I approached it, I remembered the years that Jim and I had lived in the Mexican Town neighborhood nearby after we got married. Jim had been in medical school at Wayne State, and I was working at Henry Ford Hospital in the city and taking classes toward a graduate degree. The street that we lived on, Vinewood, crossed West Fort Street that I hiked to pass underneath the bridge. Our years in the city had been happy and busy, years filled with light.

I walked underneath the Ambassador Bridge that stitched Detroit with Windsor, Ontario, and made my way on into the heart of downtown. The steady wind I had battled all day blew even faster in the canyons between skyscrapers. I found my hotel and was blown into the revolving door. I pushed a half circle inside and stepped into the stillness there, my ears still ringing from the rushing of the wind.


## The original Water Works and a walk by the river

Watching the weather forecast, I noticed a prediction of a nasty dip in the temperature the day after next. It would be accompanied by snow, sleet, and generalized cold that would seep into your bones. Since I had a little slack in my schedule, I decided to take this extra-cold day off. The first day, I would take a cab fifteen miles north of my hotel and hike back into the heart of Detroit. This allowed me to stay several nights at the same place, something I always appreciated.

After the cab dropped me off, I caught glimpses of Lake Saint Clair as

I hiked southward through the well-heeled Grosse Point neighborhoods back toward Detroit, but large houses populated the shoreline, blocking most views. When I eventually stepped over the border and crossed back into the city, it felt like someone had turned off the money switch. The buildings sagged, the streets cracked, the houses looked a little sad.

I walked Jefferson Avenue as it wound its way through the city, passing by the old Water Works Park (renamed Gladwin Park), a gated and restricted area that abuts the river. This was the first pumping station for Detroit's water, built in 1879 and the sole water source for the city until 1914. This land was much more than a pumping station in the past, though. It was a lushly green park of over 100 acres that citizens of Detroit would flock to for recreation. There are postcards and photos from those early days; one from the 1930s shows the lagoon filled with people wading to cool off. An earlier one from the turn of the century shows women in long, bustled dresses and men in suits and ties – everyone wearing hats – strolling the grounds which included a floral clock. There were tennis courts, picnic areas, a baseball diamond, and playgrounds. Children would float toy boats in the lagoon. It was a place of beauty, the place Detroiters took visitors to show off their city.

Pear trees that dated back to when the French settled the area once lined the banks of the Detroit River. A grove of a dozen, affectionately called the "Twelve Apostles," thrived in the park. The last one died around 1940. It was more than 200 years old, and its trunk had grown to be more than 4 feet in diameter. Descendants of these trees still grow on both sides of the river.

Security concerns for the city's water supply closed the park during both World Wars. Then, in 1951, the entire site was closed. Citizens of Detroit demonstrated to get their park back, and a few acres were opened to the public for a few years before the entire site was fenced off forever.

There is an ornate, marble gate that was once the main entrance to the park. It is festooned with carvings, and a marble eagle spreads its wings on the highest point in the grand Victorian tradition. It looks magnificent and noble, as if it should stand on a grand boulevard in Paris. Here, it is now the entryway to nowhere, a deserted piece of land whose apex of glory is remembered by few still living, a place so long abandoned in a city so far back on its heels it doesn't have time to curate and maintain the story of its past.

I have a personal connection to Detroit, those years Jim and I lived and worked within its boundaries, those years living within sight of the bridge and so close to the old Detroit Tiger's stadium that we could hear the cheers from our elevated back porch. If we listened to the game on the radio, the broadcasted cheers would be echoed an instant later by the live cheers drifting toward us from the stadium in the distance.

In between, the old train station, Michigan Central Station, stood its ground as it had since 1914. It was abandoned even back when we lived there. It still stands today in that spot, a ruin saved from demolition by being listed on the Register of Historic Places. It was the tallest train station in the world when built, designed in the Beaux Arts Classical style by the same firm that designed New York's Grand Central Station. Most of the windows have been broken long ago; wind rushes through this building that is steeped in such history. Dreamers spread rumors of a future for this structure, but the last time it was useful was for an episode of a television cop drama. The decay of Detroit was personified by having a detective chase a suspect through this abandoned, hulking edifice.

I still harbor much affection for this city. On my hike I was looking for any glimmer of hope for Detroit, any gathering of people who cared about the city, any project underway pointing to a brighter future for this once grand city. A public/private partnership under the name Detroit RiverFront Conservancy has worked for almost a decade to reclaim and return riverfront access to the people. As I hiked along Jefferson Avenue, I reached Gabriel Richard Park at the bridge to Belle Isle.

Here I walked a stretch of the new RiverWalk. Belle Isle is, itself, an urban park with many opportunities to escape the city. There are paths and baseball diamonds, places to fish, and a historic plant conservatory. There used to be an aquarium and a small zoo, but they were closed under Kwame Kilpatrick's reign as Mayor (before he was thrown in jail).

Frederick Law Olmstead created the master plan for the landscape of the island. You probably know him for some of the other famous parks he designed like Central Park in New York and Jackson Park in Chicago and Lake Park in Milwaukee. Today, the Detroit riverfront had been transformed, paved and tamed, and there were colorful banners and signs decorating the area, but few people. I saw a young father teaching his kids how to fish here, but otherwise it was deserted.

I had to walk a series of streets to the next part of the walkway, and in doing so passed torn-up lots where buildings had been pulled out by their roots. Some of the riverfront has gone wild with dense weeds, and most of the undeveloped land was fenced off, some of it awaiting a cleanup of toxic substances persisting there.

The longest length of the RiverWalk stretches from Rivard Street all the way to Joe Louis Arena, and they did a beautiful job here in design and execution. There are large flower gardens, sculpture installations, fountains that spring from the walkway. Here, people were enjoying the area even as rain clouds gathered over the city. I walked this long stretch watching all the people: couples holding hands, families riding bikes along the wide paths, kids running around. Finally, some life in the city, some hope.

I noticed a man fishing in the river, his bicycle and fish bucket nearby. I walked over and peered into the bucket. Five large perch were in there, so freshly caught they were still gasping.

"Nice catch!" I congratulated him on his success, as I leaned on the railing near him and gazed out on the river. We chatted for a long while, and Ronnie told me he had lived in the city for over 30 years.

"How do you think Detroit's doing?" I asked.

"Oh, it's coming back. I think Mayor Bing is a good guy, lots better than Kwame," he said as he reeled in his line, checked his bait, and recast.

"Can't get much worse than Kwame," I noted. Mayor Kwame Kilpatrick had abused his power in many creative ways until he was finally tossed in jail.

Ronnie chuckled and nodded. We talked politics a bit, and he quoted the adage about absolute power corrupting absolutely.

"I think people are basically good," he said, "but sometimes they go rotten." He turned his back to the river and considered the skyline of Detroit. "Yep. I think it's coming back. This city's not over yet."

I thanked him for the conversation and for his optimism, and left him to his fishing as I finished my walk for the day, returning to my hotel as rain began to fall from the sky.


## A day off or "Take Me Out to the Ballpark"?

My plan for the cold, blustery day was to take a break. I was eager to order room service for breakfast, stay in my robe all day, watch TV and catch up on movies while snuggled underneath the covers. I'd cocoon all day, then have dinner with Les and Milene at my hotel when they drove downtown to meet me after their workdays. I wouldn't go outdoors at all, all day!

Just as I finished my breakfast, my cell rang.

It was Leslie and she sounded excited. "I got tickets for the Tiger game," she said. "Milene and I will be there around one to pick you up!"

I looked down at the fluffy robe I was wearing, then at the window. Sleet was pitter-pattering on the glass.

"Okay," I managed.

"Yay! See you soon."

I poured myself another cup of coffee and climbed into bed. I had the morning, at least, before I would have to layer up in order to go to a base-ball game in the snow. In the *snow!*

They arrived at the hotel driving Milene's yellow Jeep. They were giddy with the excitement of playing hooky from work and escaping to the city. They were wearing winter coats and gloves and scarves. We drove the short distance to the ballpark and found our seats. We were directly behind the dugout, first row. We used the top of the dugout to rest our hotdogs and hot chocolate. When little snowballs began pattering off of our hoods, we laughed at the absurdity of baseball being played in the snow.

"Whose idea was this?" I laughed.

The stadium protected us from the swirling winds, and the Tigers man-aged to win the game. Leslie kept reapplying her lipstick since she was sure we would be seen on the television broadcast.

After the game, we went to nearby Greektown for dinner before they had to head home. The day was an extraordinary and delightful respite from the solitude of the hike with two of my favorite people. And the con-versation was worlds better than what my backpack was providing.

## Mandatory art diversion

I couldn't leave Detroit before visiting one of my favorite places: The Diego Rivera atrium at the Detroit Institute of Art. Henry Ford's son, Edsel Ford, commissioned the Mexican painter Rivera to paint frescos depicting the auto industry on one wall of this atrium. After Rivera saw the space, he planned to use it all. He toured the Rouge plant and other facilities around Detroit with a photographer for three months, then he used the photos to develop his sketches for the frescos. It would take him eleven months to fill the room with his masterwork. It is signed and dated by him, completed in 1933.

Sunlight streamed in through the glass ceiling while he worked. Rivera lost over 100 pounds while painting here; he put himself into these frescos and they are magnificent. The four walls contain more than a depiction of industry. There are layers of philosophy, religion, politics, science, and workers rights. The colors, even after decades, are vibrant.

The murals were controversial when they were completed. Some people called them blasphemous, incendiary, or even pornographic (since there were archetypal women depicting the various races who had bare breasts). There was a call for the murals to be destroyed, for the limestone plaster to be jackhammered from the walls of this art institute.

Edsel Ford had funded the mural and stood by its preservation. He was quoted as saying, simply, "I like it."

As I mentioned, my grandpa worked at the Rouge and was there when Rivera toured the plant. The first thing I noticed the first time I saw the fresco as a kid was an assembly-line worker that looks just like my grandpa. At the time Rivera toured, there would have been tens of thousands of workers at the complex, but still, it's nice to think he may have captured a bit of my family's history in this masterpiece.

After visiting the fresco, I gathered my backpack from the hotel and took a cab back up to Grosse Pointe Farms (the place where I had been dropped off to hike back into Detroit to my hotel two days earlier) and headed north to Mount Clemens along the edge of Lake St. Clair. There were short stretches where the shoreline was accessible for my walking. The longest stretch was at the beginning from Pier Park to the Grosse Pointe Yacht Club. Lake Shore Road hugs Lake St. Clair for this stretch where the lake begins to funnel into the Detroit River. Phragmites – an invasive grass that grows over 12 feet tall – grew in patches along the shore, but the shoulder of the road elevated me over most of it so I could see out into the lake.

Lake St. Clair averages only eleven feet deep, so a shipping channel has been dredged to accommodate lake freighters moving between lakes Erie and Huron. A tugboat chugged north in this channel as I walked. Water moves quickly through Lake St. Clair, taking only days to go from the northern end at the St. Clair River to enter the Detroit River to the south.

## The death of Tecumseh

I could see the Canadian shoreline along much of the horizon since the shallow lake is only about 20 miles across at its widest point. It was on the other side of this small body of water that Tecumseh was slain in battle. His blood was spilled on land that he had no interest in; he only wanted to restore his homeland to his people in what is now the state of Ohio. The British commander at this battle, Proctor, slunk away from the fight unharmed. He was later reprimanded for his conduct, for abandoning the native warriors who so valiantly fought at his side.

Americans have come to recognize what an extraordinary man Tecumseh had been. There are towns, roads, buildings, warships, and monuments named after him. General William Tecumseh Sherman, one of the most famous generals in the Civil War, carried the warrior chief's name around with him as his middle name. Probably the biggest acknowledgement of Tecumseh's role in American history is the fresco depicting his death. It is one of the scenes painted in the "Frieze of American History" that runs below the row of windows in the rotunda of the U.S. Capitol building in Washington D.C. The Death of Tecumseh is alongside scenes of the Landing of Columbus, the Signing of the Declaration of Independence, Peace at the End of the Civil War, and the Birth of Aviation (among others).

Approaching the Grosse Pointe Yacht Club, I was struck by how its slender tower resembled a minaret with its cone-shaped roof and balcony. Mansions lined the other side of the road with unobstructed views of the lake. Gardeners trimmed and mowed the grand lawns as I hiked. North of the yacht club, the shoreline was given over to private houses, and I had to hike the sidewalk nearby, catching only fleeting glimpses of the water where it had not been fenced or obscured by the sprawling, beautiful homes. Along the route I passed the estate of Edsel and Eleanor Ford. It is now a museum. I nodded my thanks to Mr. Ford for commissioning and defending the Rivera frescoes, then continued hiking north.

## Yikes! Nothing like the stock photos!

I arrived in Mt. Clemens and headed toward my hotel. A good friend of mine, Maija, lives in the northern suburbs of Detroit. She was planning to meet up with me at my motel that evening and take me out to dinner.

I found the motel – a small, roadside, one-story structure. I had stayed at many "mom-and-pop" establishments on my previous hike and had pretty good experiences. These motels were usually a little worn around the edges and the décor was dated, but they were generally clean and safe, a good place to crash after a day of hiking with a heavy pack.

This motel had a glossy website, complete with photos of a maid in uniform fluffing pillows and images of a modern bathroom with glassed-in shower. I knew these were stock photos, but figured they had to be at least an approximate representation of this little motel, and I remained hopeful as I entered the office. When I saw the security enclosure for the owner, I had my first doubts about the place. I pressed a doorbell button and a tiny woman emerged from a door inside the enclosure. She was draped in a beautiful sari and the office smelled of exotic spices.

"I called about a room?" When I gave her my name, she looked at me blankly, so I said, "One room, one night?" and held up one finger.

She nodded and said, "Forty." I slipped the cash into the metal tray, and she chose a key from the hooks on the wall and traded it for the cash. She made a circular motion with her hand and said, "Around back."

"Thanks," I said as I headed out of the office. Walking around the building, I noticed the battered cars parked there, the dumpster overflowing with shattered furniture and old countertops. *Maybe they're renovating,* I thought, trying to remain hopeful.

I went around the back of the building and saw that beyond the motel was a feral field strewn with trash. A van was parked there; it was missing a couple of windows that were taped over with garbage bags. As I approached my room, I noticed that all windows had been replaced with glass blocks. For security reasons, I assumed. Still clinging to the hope that the room would be fine and my backpack and I could lock ourselves in and rest, I slipped the key into the door handle and turned.

I pushed the door in and stepped into the cloying, smoky interior. And it wasn't cigarette smoke . . . or marijuana . . . it was something denser, and it seemed to envelop and cling to me. The bed was swaybacked, the carpet matted and dirty. I glanced into the bathroom. No, it was not anything like the stock photo – oh my, not even on the same planet! – and I quickly stepped back outside. I took care to lock the door before I walked back to the office.

This is the place, I realized, that you move to after you've lost everything due to your meth addiction and have now decided to *cook* meth.

I rang for the tiny woman and she reappeared. I tried to explain that I wasn't going to stay, and she held up another key.

"Not another room," I said. "Money." I pushed my key farther into the metal tray. "Not staying."

She looked at me blankly.

"Money," I said again, firmly but not unkindly.

She disappeared through the door inside. I wondered what I'd do if she did not return. Would it be worth the hassle of calling the police? She returned with cash in her hand before I had to make that decision. I thanked her and walked on.

I knew there were other places to stay, so I stopped and managed to locate one on the river farther ahead. I called. No one answered, so I decided to just walk there, another three miles. I called Maija on the way and gave her the new address.

When I got to the next hotel, it looked better than the previous one. I entered the office, which was again fitted with a security enclosure for the worker. I looked around for a buzzer when a woman emerged from the darkness inside the booth and scared the hell out of me.

"Yikes! I didn't see you there," I said. "I left a message earlier about a room for tonight? No one called me back."

"Yeah," she slurred, "We're pretty bad at that."

The office reeked of smoke, so I asked, "Do you have non-smoking rooms?"

She slowly shook her head.

I had noticed tall stacks of little square packets on her side of the booth, but it was in this moment that I realized what they were: condoms. Stacks of various types of condoms.

"I'm going to think about it, okay?" I said as I backed out of the office.

When Maija arrived a short while later, she parked and began getting out of her car. I waved her off, "We're not staying!" I almost yelled as my backpack and I squished into the passenger seat. She started the engine and pulled out of the lot.

"You're not staying here?"

"Nope. I think they're running a brothel or something," I said. "They've got stacks of condoms inside the office. Have you ever seen that? I've never seen that!"

"Yikes," Maija said.

Consulting the Internet, I called several motels and B&Bs along Anchor Bay on the north side of Lake St. Clair. Since Maija had a car, I hoped to take a little hop around Selfridge Air National Guard base, and back to the water. No one answered at any of the places I called, so I left messages where I could as we drove to the city of New Baltimore on Anchor Bay. With the sun getting low on the horizon, I called one more B&B in Marine City on the St. Clair River about fifteen miles east of our restaurant. No one answered, so I left a message.

Undaunted, Maija and I had a nice dinner and caught up on our families and busy lives.

In a pause in our talking and eating, she looked at me. "So . . . where am I dropping you?"

"Well, if no one calls me back, you'll be taking me home with you," I laughed.

As we were finishing dinner, my cell phone rang. Finally, a place to stay. It was the one farthest away, a gorgeous B&B in Marine City on the banks of the St. Clair River.

Since my left hip had been bothering me for the last fifty miles or so, I decided to stay two nights in Marine City, walk the riverfront south a bit, and try to find a chiropractor who would work out some of the kinks in my back and hip. The chiropractor I found was a good guy who not only worked me into his schedule the following day, but also the final morning before I resumed my hike north. He also gave me some stretches to do.

"How do you warm up before you begin hiking each morning," he asked.

"Ah . . . I just walk. If things are tight, I walk it off," I said.

"Well . . . how's that working for you?" he laughed.

"Not great," I had to admit.

He used a percussive massager on my muscles – kind of like a rubber-tipped jackhammer – and showed me several stretches that I would do throughout the rest of the hike to prevent the muscles in my upper thigh and hip from shortening and causing trouble later on.

In the time I had to walk around Marine City, I felt like I had traveled back in time. The downtown is quaint and the buildings well kept. On the side of one establishment, I could see the ghost of a mural, advertising a hardware store that used to occupy the corner building. A ferry crosses the river here from Canada to Marine City, a lovely way to cross the border when the bridges are backed up.

Then, I was on my way again. As I hiked north, I used the "Bay to Bridge" designated route most of the way, watching many lake freighters glide by on their way up or down the river. I was used to seeing freighters out on the big lake, little toy ships on the horizon, but in the river they loomed tall and enormous. I wondered how they slipped up and down the river without running aground.

I had heard it wasn't always smooth passage. "Oh, you know that restaurant you passed back there?" one resident had told me when I remarked on the ships navigating the narrow waterway, "The one with the deck on the river?"

I nodded.

"Well, last summer that deck was filled with people eating lunch and watching the freighters. One of the ships lost their steering. It was dropping anchors and blowing its horn and the people eating lunch thought it was something special and began waving back to the men on deck – who they could see pretty clearly, since the boat seemed to be steering right for the restaurant."

"What happened?"

"It takes a long time to stop a freighter, even in the best of circumstances. They were able to miss the restaurant, but not by much. Crushed a seawall a bit. Gave all those people quite a scare once they stopped waving back to the guys on the boat!"

## Salt from under freshwater lakes

In the city of St. Clair, a day's walk north from Marine City, I passed the Diamond Crystal Salt Company, where I was reminded of the enormous salt layer underneath the Great Lakes. It was deposited hundreds of millions of years ago when this region was covered with a shallow sea. This salt is separated from the freshwater lakes by a limestone cap. Almost half of the nation's salt – from rock salt used for water softeners, to road-salt spread to melt ice, to simple table salt – comes from under the Great Lakes region.

When Douglass Houghton, the state's first geologist and first professor of geology at the University of Michigan, was commissioned to explore the state back in the late 1830s, salt was one of the natural resources he looked for. Salt was vital to life back then, an essential commodity needed to preserve food in a time with no refrigeration. Houghton found several places where artesian wells bubbled to the surface, bringing salt with the water in a brine. These waters could be diverted to evaporating pools, where the salt could be crystalized and recovered.

The Diamond Crystal Salt Company currently uses an injection method to get the salt. They pump steam down into the salt bed to make a brine, then pull it up and evaporate the water. This process results in flakey salt crystals that deliver a lot of flavor. Fast-food restaurants are especially fond of the product.

From my hotel room that night, I looked up the St. Clair River and saw a light show. All of the industrial complexes on the Canadian side were lit up, each pipe and tube strung with lights. It was festive – in an ultra-modern, chemical-industry sort of way. This stretch of the river is called Canada's Chemical Valley. It is jammed with over 60 installations that do various industrial things like refine oil that is piped in from Alberta, or manufacture butyl rubber (the chewy part of chewing gum). One plant will soon open to manufacture bio-based succinic acid, something used in the manufacturing process of things like spandex, auto plastics, and biodegradable coffee cup lids. The presence of salt beds and the discovery of oil nearby spurred on the development of this area, and the industrial corridor has continued to thrive to this day.

This cluster of industry has not always been good stewards of the river or the land, and this area has been designated an Area of Concern by the EPA. Long-term health studies on the First Nation peoples in the area demonstrate the toll extracted on the people who live in the shadow of this complex. Within that population, there are many health problems, including increases in autoimmune diseases and asthma. Most curiously, birth statistics are becoming increasingly skewed: of all the live births in the community, there are two girls born for every boy.

## Edison and Acheson

The city of Port Huron is plastered with references to Thomas Edison. He spent his boyhood (from seven to the age of sixteen) here. His father was a bit of a rebel, and the family had to flee from Canada to Michigan when Thomas was younger.

I know! How many people have you heard of who have had to flee Canada?

Turns out there were a couple brief rebellions against the British Crown, and Thomas's father took part in one. Most Canadians at the time were pretty happy with the relationship with Britain, and so the rebels were either jailed or fled the country. The Edison family settled in Michigan.

While Port Huron is still proud of their connection to Thomas Edison, it was not mutual. Edison spoke smack about the city his entire life; he once wrote a letter encouraging his aging father to leave the city. The Edison family had a rough time in Port Huron during the Civil War since they sympathized with the American South. It seems they were always living in the wrong region for their politics.

At some point, Edison's dislike for the city must have tempered a bit, because when his friend and former employee, Dr. Edward Goodrich Acheson, was looking for a place to establish his research facility, Edison suggested Port Huron. Acheson helped develop the filaments for Edison's light bulbs. He left Edison's company to continue his own research with electricity and found a way to manufacture graphite and improve on lubricants for industry, and he created an extremely hard abrasive he called "Carborundum."

Acheson's company still exists in Port Huron; Acheson Industries is the headquarters for worldwide operations. This company holds many patents all over the world. Some of the heirs of this fortune still reside in Port Huron and have supported the city's growth and improvement.

One such investment is in the redevelopment of land held by Acheson Ventures along the St. Clair River. They are transforming this tract of land into the Great Lakes Maritime Center. They built Vantage Point there, a gathering place to watch the freighters moving up and down the river. The building itself is rectangular and from the back looks like a massive mobile home.

When I arrived, I walked up wooden steps to a set of glass doors and stepped inside. The entire wall facing the river is also glass. The floor is carpeted, with welcoming tables set up the length of the building, with great views of the river. Most of the tables were filled with people, some working on laptops, others playing cards, others just staring out at the river.

I went to the information desk, unhooked my white backpack and leaned it against the desk along with my hiking pole, and introduced myself. The three volunteers there – Marlene, Ellen, and Mary – gathered to fill me in about the center. They told me that over 300,000 people had visited the previous year, including travelers from as far away as England and Scotland, New Zealand, Korea and Japan.

"We've worked to make this not only a tourist destination," Marlene said, "but also a hub for the community."

"We have a farmer's market here throughout the summer and a flower show in May," Ellen added.

"And we run programs for the kids," Mary said. "Teach them how to fish, or let them build a bird house. We get a lot of kids here on those days."

When a murmur went through the room, Mary excused herself and picked up a microphone. It turned out that they announce each freighter as it passes by: its name, what flag it flies, what cargo it carries, where it got the cargo, and its destination. The ships pass so close to the near riverbank that we could easily hear the thrumming of the engines. When I spread my hand out on the tabletop, it was vibrating. There was a deck on the river-side of the center, and some people moved outside to get a closer look or to take photos of the ship. The men walking around on the freighter deck were distinct and snapped the size of the enormous ship to scale with their tiny presence.

After the announcement was finished, I wanted to applaud. The passing of each ship was like a wonderfully theatrical performance: "Commerce on the Great Lakes" or "Shipping Up Close." These massive ships transport cargo like petroleum, coal, steel coils, grain, potash, limestone and taconite pellets (a partially refined form of iron ore) up and down the lakes. If it was announced that a ship was "in ballast" that meant it was empty, on its way to pick up cargo. I discovered that there are around 200 of these behemoths on the lakes at any given time.

I thanked the volunteers and wandered around the center a bit. Old photos of this area before it was reimagined and reinvigorated hung on the walls. The location used to be an enormous train yard, a place to hold trains before they traveled through a tunnel that stretched underneath the river. This passageway, completed in 1891, was the world's first, full-sized tunnel that ran underneath water; it was an engineering marvel at the time. Eventually, a new, larger tunnel was completed a century later to handle the increase in train traffic between Canada and the U.S. here.

Vantage Point has two large, flat screen monitors. One displays a satellite image of the area with real-time locations and names of freighters within a hundred miles or so of Port Huron, either north of the city on Lake Huron, or south, on the St. Clair River. On the other screen is a list of these ships and the estimated time they will glide by the window.

I made my way over to the snack bar and ordered two donuts and a large juice. I had a few more miles to hike this day, but I wanted to see at least one more ship pass by. I am also not against eating a couple of donuts after hiking all day.

## A magic trick with a lake freighter

An acquaintance of mine who had grown up in Port Huron told me I had to do something in particular while I was walking through the town. "Stand underneath the bridge," he wrote, "and watch a freighter enter the river.

"The current on one side is much faster than the other, so the ships have to enter near the Canadian shore, slide across to the American shore, then make a sharp turn east as the river curves." This didn't sound all that exciting until I read the next sentence. "If you stand there while it passes, you will see *all four sides of the ship.*"

Now, I had seen the size of these freighters and the width of the river, and this seemed impossible, like this slight-of-hand on a freighter-sized scale could only be pulled off by David Copperfield, perched on the bow of the ship, laughing manically.

This, I had to see.

I hiked in the early morning light along Port Huron's lovely riverwalk until I reached the bridge. A freighter was bound to come by soon, so I waited. I had been over the Blue Water Bridge a few times in my life. Crossing the border can be hectic and stressful if it was crowded or if the customs officer was having anger issues, so I had never fully appreciated the beauty of the bridge.

The best view of most bridges is from underneath, anyway, and this bridge with its elegant arches of steel spanning the river in one neat leap is gorgeous. The river is a beautiful blue here, almost aqua, due to the current picking up and suspending glacial till and clay in the water.

Seeing my backpack, a few joggers on the riverwalk stopped to ask me how far I was hiking.

"Oh, I'm doing a thousand miles this year. I started down in Ohio."

We would chat a bit – they often asked if I had hiked through Detroit – then they'd jog off down the river. Port Huron's riverwalk reminded me of Detroit's. I am amazed how people are continually drawn to the water, and if you give them access – a beach, a park, a lovely riverwalk – they will come to the water's edge. It must be a primal need we have to be near this elemental liquid, to watch it flow, to move alongside it.

There is a statue of Edison in the park underneath the bridge. The statue portrays him with a broad smile, though I'm pretty sure he would not be quite so thrilled to be back in this town where he spent his unhappy youth. I snapped a couple photos of him and the bridge, then noticed a freighter navigating toward the mouth of the river. As I stood there, I saw the bow and starboard (right) side of the boat. It lined up parallel to the Canadian shoreline. I looked at the surface of the river and could see that the water nearest me was moving much faster than the water near the far shore.

The ship headed directly toward me, seemingly intent to run aground at my feet, but as it crossed the river, it made a sweeping turn to enter the faster current and ride that down the river and through the curve. The ship passed so close to me I could have tossed a rock and struck the iron wall of the ship's side.

Magically, as the ship made the turn, I saw the stern of the ship, then the port (left) side. Quite a trick, and one I would not have believed if I hadn't seen it for myself.

David Copperfield was nowhere in sight.

My pack and I set off north, heading to the second Great Lake on my hike, Lake Huron.

I had just hiked the most elaborate connection between the lakes. The Detroit River, Lake St. Clair, and the St. Clair River connect lakes Huron and Erie. This waterway stretches almost 100 miles. Industry and cities are concentrated along these sheltered stretches. Jobs are concentrated here. And decades of pollution have also been dumped and deposited in these waterways.

## Seawalls and rocky shoals

After hiking for five days along these connecting waters, I was thrilled to get back to the shores of a Great Lake, to see the open expanse of water. Lake Huron opened up in front of me after I passed underneath the Blue Water Bridge. I found myself smiling and walking a little faster. I first had to hike around Fort Gratiot Lighthouse, the oldest lighthouse in the state of Michigan. It was undergoing renovation at the time and was fenced off so the shoreline was inaccessible, but I soon returned to the beach that continued north of the light.

I had expected wide, open beaches for at least a few miles, but many homeowners had installed tall seawalls along their property lines, perpendicular to the shore and reaching out into the lake. These barriers were rusted, corrugated steel that had been driven down into the sand and then topped with a flat piece of steel. They were rusty-brown in color, solid, and extended out into the lake with the purpose of calming the waves and holding onto the shoreline.

Some were easy to get past if they were buried deep enough in the sand, leaving only a few feet popping up away from the water's edge. I would just hop over these, or jump up onto the flat top and swing my legs over the other side and hop down. But I soon came upon a series of walls that was over six feet on the land side, reaching out into the lake into knee-deep water. I was up to the challenge. Digging into my pack, I pulled out a couple of ever-versatile trash bags. I stepped into them, hoisted my pack again, and, using the bags as waders, trudged into the lake and around the far ends of the taller seawalls.

I pushed onward and was soon walking in Lakeside Park where the beach was blissfully unobstructed. When it began to rain, I reached a large stream cutting across the shore and merging with the lake, so I headed inland to walk the road for a bit. When it began to pour, I found a community center with a covered porch with a couple of plastic chairs and my pack and I took a break, watching and waiting patiently while the clouds drained.

You'd think that backpack manufacturers would have considered that backpacks, at times, would be outside in the weather and maybe make them waterproof. The last time I looked at new backpacks, they had finally managed this mental leap; packs now are often constructed with a rubberized coating, at least on the very top of the pack. Mine was manufactured pre-weather epiphany, though, so I had to cover it with a trash bag anytime it rained very hard to keep the water from seeping inside to my gear.

## The thumb

In the many days that I hiked up the outer edge of Michigan's thumb, several questions arose in my mind: Where were all the rivers? Why was it so flat? And why was it so unpopulated?

This topography was nothing like the western edge of the state where I had walked the sandy edge of Lake Michigan on my first hike. To understand why two sides of the same state can be so different, one has to return to a time long ago when the Great Lakes were forming as the last of the ice sheets retreated. The thumb of Michigan remained submerged in shallow water, after the rest of the Lower Peninsula had shed its ice. As it rose, slowing rebounding from the weight of the ice, water had to drain off the non-thumb part of the state, which led to a vast network of streams and rivers. Meanwhile, the thumb, still submerged, was being leveled out by the action of the water that covered it. It was only when the Great Lakes shrank inside their current boundaries that the thumb was finally above water again. The water near the land here is often shallow and rocky for long stretches out into Lake Huron. These shoals make for treacherous boating.

Other questions that came to my mind (on a long hike, you have lots of time to think about any number of odd things) had to do with all the bowling alleys and quilting places I saw in each town. What's with all the quilting and bowling in the thumb? Are they separate and distinct groups? Or do quilters bowl? Do bowlers quilt? How much crossover was there between the two activities?

What did *that* Venn diagram look like?

If you look up information about the famous White Rock that sits about a quarter mile offshore in Lake Huron just south of the town of Harbor Beach, you'll learn how it was used as a marker in a treaty where Native Americans ceded land for settlers. In the 1805 agreement, the encroaching settlers were prohibited from travel north of this marker. This information is true, but it skips over the deeper significance of White Rock. Back when the most efficient way to travel in the Great Lakes region was on the lakes, and since the land was heavily wooded and pretty uniform in this area – with no great rivers to mark the shoreline – something like an extra-large white rock sitting out in the lake was a welcome navigational aid. Native Americans not only used it as a geographical marker, but also revered it as a holy site.

There is a roadside park today at the rock. The White Rock is about a half mile out in a shoal and rises about four feet above the water. It is twelve feet square. Wave action, harsh winters, lightning strikes, and being used by the Air Force for target practice with dummy bombs have all diminished it over time, but it is still pretty remarkable when looking out from the bluff. There is a long staircase leading down to the beach, so I descended to see the rock from lake level.

The signs at the park retold a tale from the mid-1800s. A group of white settlers decided to go out to the rock and dance on it. A Native American warned them not to degrade the sacred rock this way, but most of them waded out to the rock anyway. One person heeded the warning, and this guy was standing with the Native American watching as the others began dancing on the rock. It must have seemed like a lot of fun – until lightning struck the rock, killing all the dancers.

The town of White Rock was destroyed by the Great Fire of 1871, a conflagration that burned up most of Michigan's thumb. This was part of the same regional weather system and ultra-dry conditions (and in many cases fed by the abundance of dry refuse from the timbering industry) that led to the simultaneous great fires that destroyed Chicago, the Peshtigo regions of Wisconsin, along with smaller fires in the Western Michigan cities of Manistee, Holland and Grand Rapids. The fact that most of these fires started the same day have led some to speculate about whether there was a common ignition source. A disintegrating comet – which was passing Earth that October – has intrigued some fire conspiracy theorists as a possible cause, but that's deemed highly unlikely.

The Chicago History Museum has an entire display related to The Great Chicago Fire with many artifacts that tell the tale of the intense firestorm that swept the city. There are glass jars and bottles that melted from the heat of the fire, bending and slumping. A child's collection of colorful marbles melded together is on display. The fire was so hot it even melted metal: blobs on display can be identified as a pile of washers or screws fused from the heat.

Most people recall The Great Chicago Fire, but that was not the largest or most destructive fire that day. It's just that there were more people who survived the Chicago fire to tell the tale. Multiple fires devastated the region, killing thousands and consuming property and crops and structures on a scale not experienced before (or since) in this country.

The fire that charred Michigan's thumb was so all-consuming that an organization was created to help the people displaced by it, to come to their aid. It is an organization that is still around today. You've probably heard of it: The American Red Cross.

That day, I hiked nine more miles north of the White Rock along the outer edge of Michigan's thumb to the town of Harbor Beach. Along the way, I contemplated this land being engulfed in flames, the people fleeing into Lake Huron, wading out into the rocky shallows and turning back to see the wall of flames swallowing everything – their homes, their crops . . . everything but their lives. If they were the lucky ones.

Steam travel came to the Great Lakes in the mid-1800s. Prior to that, sails filled the lakes during the mild months as people and goods moved through the region. As noted, given the shallowness of the waters in this part of the lake, sailing around the thumb could be a gamble with your vessel and life. Ships leaving Saginaw Bay (in the crook of the thumb) had no port of refuge, no safe harbor, until they reached the St. Clair River over 100 miles away. If a storm caught them while on route, they either had to fight their way back to Saginaw Bay – usually against the wind – or high-tail it with the wind to Port Huron and the mouth of the St. Clair River.

Thousands of small ships were unsuccessful in finding refuge over the years, and after many ships and lives were lost, the Army Corps of Engineers were commissioned to build an artificial harbor in between the two natural ones. They chose the town of Sand Beach (now called Harbor Beach) and set about building the largest manmade harbor in the world. The breakwall enclosed a watery refuge of over 600 acres. Between when it was built and the turn of the twentieth century, there were over 50,000 visits from ships that sought shelter here, with countless lives saved.

## Waving . . .

Long stretches that I had to trudge along highway M-25, due to impassable stretches of shoreline, led to some moments of, well, abject boredom and imagined conversations with my backpack. No people, few houses, sparse cars passing me by. This situation led to my habit of waving . . .

. . . to cows.

Cows, you see, are social animals. They live in herds and hang out together. Unlike horses who spend most of their time eating, cows take breaks to chew their cuds, reworking stuff eaten earlier. This gives them time to ruminate (yes, I just said that) and look around for newsworthy happenings and new friends. This is the time you want to wave to them and maybe even give a jaunty "Hello!"

I've had cows get to their feet when they saw my friendly greeting and amble over to the fence to let me rub their foreheads between their eyes. This is the social contract with cows: if they come over, you *must* rub that broad spot between their eyes.

With horses it's different. Since they have only one stomach, they are constantly hungry. If they come to the fence they expect some food, so pull up some tall grass as you make your way to greet them.

After another fifteen miles of hiking, I caught my first glimpse of the tallest lighthouse I would see during this month's hike. It is called the Pointe aux Barques Lighthouse. This is French for "Point of Little Boats." The lighthouse is well preserved and has a lovely park and campground around it. The museum wasn't open yet, but I let my pack rest on the porch while I walked around the grounds a bit.

The day was very windy, and since I was nearing the tip of the thumb, the waves were kicking up with the weather. I made my way to the shoreline and found huge rocks breaking the waves into spray along the edge of the land. Returning to my pack, I pulled a small cigar out of one of its pockets and returned to the water. I crumbled it into the wind and watched the dry leaves get swooped up and cast out onto the water. An offering of tobacco is what the Native Americans used to give to the lakes as thanks for safe passage. I had hiked a long way this month – over 200 miles at this point – and still had a long way to go this year before my journey would be complete.

I was thankful that I had the time and energy to undertake this adventure and hoped the lakes would continue to grace my journey with safe passage.

## Tip-o-the-Thumb

As I walked on, I saw developments named "Tip-o-the-Thumb," so I knew I was nearing the top of that rounded peninsula that forms the thumb of Michigan's mitten shape.

There was a batch of interesting things in this area. The first is Grindstone City. It was in the quarry here that excellent sandstone (part of the Marshall formation) was extracted and shaped into millstones – used to grind grain – and to manufacture the premier honing stones for sharpening tools and knives. I passed many houses and campgrounds that had old millstones propped in the front yard or as a decoration in a flowerbed. Some of these stones were quite big, taller than me. My route took me past the old quarry. I hiked over to look down into the abandoned pits now lined with the rubble left over from the operation.

It certainly was a labor-intensive process to mine and shape the grindstones. Once a slab of stone was carefully drilled and released from the quarry walls, the men would soak it in water to make it easy to shape. They'd chisel a square hole through the middle and slide it onto a metal bar. A steam engine would then turn the stone, and two men – one on either side of the whirling sandstone slab – would shape it with metal tools until they produced a symmetrical, balanced, grinding stone.

Grindstone City was a thriving community for nearly a century and the excellent millstones shaped there found a market all over the world, then the town abruptly died. Why? Remember Edison's friend, Acheson? The guy working with electricity and carbon? One of his creations, Carborundum, was developed in the search for artificial diamonds. And this creation turned out to be an excellent abrasive. So excellent, in fact, that they could manufacture grinding stones and millstones out of it. And they could do it at a lower cost than the operation at Grindstone City. Thus, Grindstone City became a ghost town almost overnight.

Speaking of ghost towns, there is a historic village at the tip of the thumb called Huron City. Old buildings – houses, churches, meeting places – have been moved there and arranged along a road for people to see. It was deserted when I walked through, like a true ghost town. Grindstones decorated many of the yards, underscoring the fact that one day these hand-hewed discs of stone became worthless, cast off for decorations, never to be put to work.

Before walking through these areas, I had ducked into a bar/party store to buy some chocolate. My chocolate stash was running low, and I didn't want to get grumpy while hiking. The store part of the establishment wasn't open for the season yet, so I ordered a coke at the bar. The television there had the Tigers baseball game on it, so I sipped my coke and thought back to the game that Leslie and Milene and I had seen earlier in the month in the snow in Detroit.

Two old gentlemen were chatting at the bar about the game, but curiosity about my backpack soon overcame them and they asked me questions, discovering I was on a long hike. We chatted a bit, then I said, "I'm off to see Grindstone City, and then the Turnip Rock."

They looked at each other quizzically.

"Can she walk in there to see the rock?" "Is the gate down?"

"There's a gate?" I asked.

"There's a guard shack, too," one of the men said. He looked at his buddy and asked, "Is Melvin working yet?"

"Not until Memorial Day," the buddy said. Then he looked at me and gave me a reassuring smile.

"You should be able to just walk in now. When the season starts they mostly keep people out."

"Yep," the other guy agreed. "Melvin won't even let us in."

The Turnip Rock sits in the lake, separated from the shoreline cliff by wave action and erosion. My friend, Sally, the artist and skull-collector, had told me she had kayaked around it. What she hadn't mentioned is that it sits within the grounds of a historic, luxury summer resort first established by the lumber barons of the thumb. This resort is called Pointe aux Barques, just like the lighthouse eleven miles to the east.

I walked along the road for about a mile, parallel to the resort's manicured golf course, and then I turned into the driveway – the guys at the bar were right: the gate was up at the resort, with no one in the guardhouse – past the tennis courts and restaurant. The place was deserted, so I plotted a route to quickly get me to the shoreline where I could see the Turnip Rock sitting out in Lake Huron.

Even from my vantage point a half-mile away, the rock was impressive. It stands about twenty feet tall, near the sandstone bluff it had once been a part of. Turnip Rock is skinnier at the bottom than the top (hence the turnip designation) and will one day topple into the lake when the bottom is worn to the point where it can no longer support its weight, balanced there in the water. A small grove of trees grows on it. Seeing this formation from a kayak would truly be the best way to grasp its scale and mass. I took many photos of the rock and the grand homes along the water's edge, then I hiked on to Port Austin.

The next day, I had just chatted with my sister Leslie on the phone, telling her how much I enjoyed the town of Port Austin when I noticed a strange thing: M-25, the road I had been on for much of the way since Port Huron, had changed from M-25 North to M-25 West. I grinned at the sign, delighted that it had recognized my progress! I had rounded the top of the "thumb" and was now making my way to the south and west toward Saginaw Bay.

I had complained to Leslie about the lack of access to the lake, but as I walked into a county roadside park and set my pack on a picnic table, I realized that, too, had now changed. To the west, a sandy shoreline stretched for miles, curving out into the lake and ending at a point far across the bay. It all looked sandy (mixed here and there with pebbles). Delightful! I knew that Port Crescent State Park was west of me and that there was a beach there, but I wasn't aware that the entire bay would be so wonderfully accessible.

Lofting my pack, I cinched all the belts and went down the grassy slope to the water's edge. I've often said that I'd rather do twenty difficult miles on soft sand by the water than ten easy miles on a roadside. Something about walking that edge rejuvenates me and connects me back to the big water. I hiked several miles into the state park, until a river winding its way through the dunes stopped my progress along the shore. It was too deep to wade, so I hiked inland over the corrugated land, its tall ridges paralleling the water. This type of landscape is indicative of glacial retreat; I walked in the footprint of the glacier.

## Sebewaing, sugar beets, and WWII

Three days of hiking a total of 58 miles from Port Austin got me to the village of Sebewaing (pronounced *SEE-ba-wing*) on Saginaw Bay on the inside of the thumb. These were three looooong days of hiking, and this area is incredibly flat, rich farmland, so when the wind blew (and I assure you, *it blew)*, I was shoved around as I walked. My bulky pack seemed to attract the wind, calling it over to toss me around even more.

There is something about hiking into a stiff wind. Not only is it more arduous, but I also felt more exposed. Maybe it was the way the wind took my breath away at times, or snuck up on me with a gust so strong I had to crouch down under my pack to keep from being blown over. Between the fatigue of hiking so many miles, being solitary for such a long stretch with only my backpack for company, and having the wind swirling around and bullying me, I felt stripped down to the essentials: hike, forward, push, move. There was an emotional exposure, a peeling away, that was unexpected.

Since the distance between Sebewaing and Bay City was beyond my 25-mile maximum to hike in a day, I arranged with Erma, the owner of the B&B in Sebewaing, to drive me to a park in between the two points. The first day, I would hike back to the B&B, the second day I would hike from the park to Bay City, the ending point for this long beginning of my adventure.

Erma had lived in Sebewaing her entire life, and since she is in her 80s, she has a long perspective on how things had changed. After I had hiked back to the B&B the first day, mostly following straight roads cutting through flat farmland (I saw the first blooming trillium of the year), she insisted on driving me around the village and the waterfront to show me important places.

Sadly, the entire waterfront was choked with phragmites. I had never seen this invasive grass grow so dense and so far out from the shore. There were places where it reached out as far as I could see and channels had to be cut through it for boats to get from the docks out to the bay. The bay was sheltered and shallow, which created perfect growing conditions for this invasive grass. I could imagine it choking off the entire bay, given enough time.

"How long has it been like this?" I asked.

"Ten years ago, there wasn't any," Erma told me. "The bay was clear. You could look out for miles. Sometimes a friend would call when all the swans came into the bay, then we'd drive over to see them. You wouldn't believe the number of swans and ducks you could see filling up the bay. And the water has gotten so much lower with all this grass. I think it's sucking the bay dry."

She drove me for miles, and the invasive grass was everywhere. If someone had had the foresight to kill it when it first appeared, it would have taken a small, concerted effort to eradicate it. Now? I couldn't imagine the resources it would take to accomplish that. I later heard of scientists using satellite images to map the spread of this invasive grass. When you can see a problem like this from space, it has probably gotten out of control.

Erma drove me by the Pioneer Sugar Plant in town. It had been there for over a century.

"I hear it smells a bit when they cook up the sugar beets in the fall," I said.

"We say that's the smell of *money.*" Erma grinned at me.

"Did you or your family ever work there?"

"Oh, as a young girl I worked in the fields one summer. It was during the war. The migrant workers didn't show up, so they pulled all the high school kids out of school to work in the fields."

"What did you have to do?"

"Well, the tractor went through first and tilled up the beets so they were mostly exposed," she said. "Have you seen a sugar beet? They're long and white, maybe a foot long?"

I nodded.

"Well, we had these long, curved blades with a special hook on the end. I have one back at the house I'll show you. We took that hook and used it to pierce and lift the beet, then we'd have to hold it in one hand and lop off the top of the beet with the curved part of the blade. The beets were too big for us girls to hold out in front of us to top, so we'd hold it against our leg. The foreman almost had a heart attack seeing us whacking away so close to our leg. Those blades were sharp! But it was the only way we could do it."

"How long did you work the fields?"

"A couple of weeks."

"Did you feel like you were doing something to support the war effort?"

"Oh . . . we thought we were wonderful," she said and broke into a broad smile. "When we returned to school, we had to make up those weeks we had missed, so it wasn't so wonderful then."

"Did some of the boys from your class fight in the war?"

Erma thought a moment. "I'm sure some did, but I don't remember. You think you'll remember everything, but you don't. It fades and disappears."

The sugar beet is responsible for the transformation of this area after the timbering industry had harvested all of the forests. There had to be a huge incentive for farmers to undertake the backbreaking task of removing the stumps left behind, and sugar beets were the premier cash crop at the beginning of the twentieth century. Farmers could move beyond subsistence with this crop, could pay off their mortgage, could get ahead. At its peak, there were over twenty factories in the state of Michigan alone producing mountains of white sugar extracted from the sugar beet.

Back at the house, Erma located a copy of the newspaper announcing the opening of the sugar plant in Sebewaing over a hundred years ago. While I read it, she searched for her turnip knife.


## Exposed

The next day, Erma drove me to the park again so I could walk the final miles to Bay City. I thanked her for her hospitality and expert chauffeur services. As I hoisted my backpack and began walking, I noticed that something was missing: the wind. The wind that had been constant while I traced the edge of the thumb along Lake Huron and Saginaw Bay had suddenly been shut off. It seemed unnatural to be outside without the wind shoving me around. I soon shed a couple of layers and found myself walking at a more leisurely pace, enjoying the sunshine and the blooming fruit trees and the beautiful trillium along the way.

The roadside ditches were filled with water choked with duckweed, and in one of them I saw a most curious sight. A six-point deer had been hit by a car and had fallen into the water. It floated there, surrounded by the bright green duckweed on the surface of the water, but the deer also had large green spots on it. As I got closer, I realized that those dots were frogs sitting on the carcass. They sat there eating the flies that were drawn to the dead deer. Since the water in the ditch was cold, the deer wasn't rotting yet, so the frogs had quite a set-up!

And I'll tell you, those frogs were chubby. They were quite happy with the all-you-could-catch-with-your-tongue fly buffet.

The day warmed, and high cirrus clouds swirled in the sky above. It was 60 degrees by the time I reached Bay City, and many of the trees lining the streets were in full bloom. I strolled along Center Avenue, past the lavish residences built by lumber barons and by sugar beet, shipping, and coal magnates. A long stretch of this street has been designated as a historical site to preserve these grand homes.

Tulips lined the sidewalk to the door of the Thomas E. Webster House, a Queen Anne style brick house that is now the Webster B&B. I climbed to the third floor and closed the door to my room behind me. I shrugged off my white backpack and set it gently on the floor. Its white color had dulled with the month of hiking through the industry and windswept farmlands.

It felt strange to take it off knowing I would not have to carry it the next day, or the next. The month of May would be taken off from the hike so I could attend Ben's graduation from college and spend some time with my boys. Lucas was heading to China to study for the summer, and I wanted to see him off on his adventure.

The room was lovely. There was a beautiful bedspread, an upholstered chair in a reading nook, and a Jacuzzi bathtub with two skylights overhead. I walked around the room for a couple of minutes, not able to sit. I touched the nice things and told myself that I could relax here for a bit, the month's hike was complete.

With the changes of the past year – the divorce, the worrying about my sons, the multiple moves, then launching out on this hike – I was feeling emotionally exposed. The wind seemed to strip away my armor, my defenses, even my strength until I felt ground down to my essential self. I couldn't settle down, and this was strange. I usually just flopped on the bed once my pack and boots were off.

I paced, still coiled against the cold and wind. I told myself it was over, that the first month of walking was done. With that thought, tears filled my eyes. I laughed, then cried, then laughed again.

Then, finally, I sat down on the floor next to my trusty backpack and leaned against it for a moment. I had carried this pack for over 300 miles, so I was sure it wouldn't mind me resting against it for a moment.

Then, I reached down and untied my boots.

The Jacuzzi tub called to me. And I was going to answer.

# June

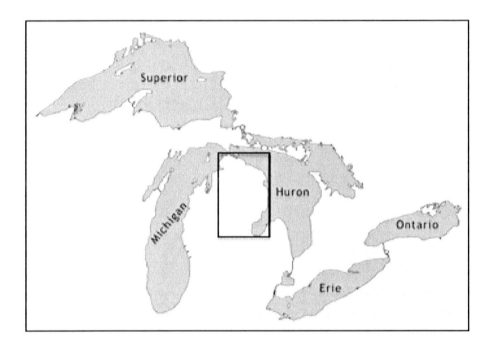

**Bay City to Harbor Springs, Michigan;
Lake Huron to Straits of Mackinac to Lake Michigan**

**303 miles in 22 days**

## Perspective

As the end of May approached, I began thinking about all the things I'd need to carry on the second part of my hike. A list of camping gear was added to my original list of essentials. When I headed back to Bay City and continued north up the eastern edge of Michigan's lower peninsula, there would be some wild and remote stretches where I would need to do some wilderness camping. I pulled out my hammock tent in its small stuff sack, then my sleeping bag, and a new, compact stove for boiling water to re-hydrate my freeze-dried meals.

When I looked at the pile of additional gear, then the regular gear, then my deflated, now-not-so-white backpack, I wondered if it would all fit. The backpack even looked dubious about the task. I combed through my choices for clothing, eliminated a few figuring that I could leave heavier pieces behind and just layer up if it got cold. I crammed things more force-fully into stuff sacks, and pulled the straps tighter on compression sacks until they were the size of volleyballs. Dense volleyballs, like volleyballs of dark matter.

Then, I wedged and stuffed and crammed everything into my backpack and filled the outer pockets with small things. Once that was done, I took hold of the upper handle on the pack with my right hand, the left shoulder strap with my left hand, and hoisted and twirled it onto my back. Cinching the waist belt and flexing my knees, I glanced back over my shoulder at the top of the pack and said, "My. Looks like one of us has gained some weight. And I know it's not me."

Ah, yes. There's nothing like the satisfaction that comes from being snarky to a backpack.

On June 1, my overstuffed pack and I took a bus from my hometown of Battle Creek back to Bay City, crossing the middle of the state. The hike would resume, now that I had completed Lake Erie's western curve and all of Michigan's thumb, and continue north from Bay City situated in the crook of Michigan's thumb on the banks of the Saginaw River.

The bus ride was a great place to people watch. There was an older man who had dressed for the trip in a baggy, burnt-orange, velour sweat suit that looked exceedingly comfortable. The velour was embossed with a letter, repeated over and over, giving him a somewhat calico appearance. He slept the entire way, and if he had licked the back of his hand to smooth out his hair after waking I would not have been surprised.

It stormed the entire ride, and strong winds pushed and pulled at the tall bus. The temperature outside struggled to get above fifty degrees. The young woman sitting next to me had recently moved back to Michigan after living for a time in Arizona.

"What brought you back?" I asked.

"The water. The trees. The color green," she said looking out onto the fields that had intensified in color with the rain. Then she told me that she had left a bad relationship out West; Michigan had called her home. "I loved the drive across the country, getting closer and closer to the Great Lakes, watching the trees spring up, everything gets greener. I knew I was home when I saw a dead deer on the side of the road. There isn't any road-kill in Arizona," she said. "Only dead tires."

She got off the bus in Lansing to meet up with friends. The bus continued through the ruins of the post-industrial city of Flint. People got on and off at most stops. The rain kept falling in sheets, and the crops in the fields lifted as they drank it in.

I had been watching one young man for much of the trip. He got on the bus early in my ride and was dressed well ahead of the fashion curve, like he had just stepped off a fashion runway. He wore skinny jeans pulled down in back to show off the top of his boxers, and rolled up at the bottom to reveal his ankles. He had on a skin-tight, flesh-colored, deep V-neck tee-shirt, and the porkpie hat on his head was adjusted to the perfect angle. His bright orange skateboard occupied the seat next to him.

This guy talked to everyone around him, deep, penetrating conversations in which he asked about people's rocky relationships and if they wrote poetry. He told an elderly woman with cornrows that he loved her braids, then she asked to see his hair and he lifted his hat to reveal his thick, wavy hair. This hipster kid seemed a little lost and way too uninhibited to be travelling alone. He spoke of being an artist and of previous careers in L.A. where he was successful, but unfulfilled. He amused me, and I found myself suppressing a smirk at some of the things he said and the way he was so open with complete strangers on a bus.

When I saw this young man's father waiting at a bus station, my entire perspective changed. The father had the same thick, wavy hair as his son, but was dressed in a conservative 3-piece suit. What snapped my perspective was the look of intense concern the father wore as he searched the faces in the bus windows for his son. When their eyes connected, the father scanned his son's face, looking for clues, I thought, as to how he was doing. Even when the son and father embraced, that worried look never left the man's face and I felt that pain, the unbreakable connection between parent and child.

By the time I got off the bus in Bay City, I had thought a long while about my own sons. About their lives and how they were both in college, both studying to be engineers. But were they happy and fulfilled with this path? Who knew what the future would bring? I had left the sciences to pursue writing. Maybe they would wander the earth a bit as this young man was doing.

Even as I was now doing.

It took me four days to hike north along the wide, western curve of Saginaw Bay. The 3,000-acre Tobico Marsh hugs the bay along this stretch. This is one of the largest remaining coastal wetlands on the Great Lakes. And even though it was logged off in the past, it was preserved pretty much unaltered after that, as the land was first sold to a hunting club and then later donated to the state. The white pines once grew to giants here: up to 175 feet tall and 7 feet in diameter.

I passed through the bayside towns of Pinconning (known for its cheese), Standish, and Au Gres. While hiking a dirt road along the Au Gres River, I saw a turtle struggling to get over the road cut and back to the water. It was a decent size, about six inches in diameter. I lifted it up and looked at it more closely. It looked worried, so I talked to it. I thought it was a painted turtle, but then noticed the intricate pattern on its shell and how its neck and upper legs were orange. This was a rare wood turtle. I studied it and chatted while walking down the bank of the river through tall weeds. I turned it loose near the water's edge, and it splashed quickly into the water.

I had arranged for the county shuttle to pick me up at the Au Gres library and take me to the county line to the north. After hiking for tens of miles on US 23 – and after a semi truck had spun a rock my way, striking and cutting my shin – I decided to take a ten mile hop on the shuttle to get me to a spot where I could hike to the end of Saginaw Bay in one day. Since only the miles I walked would be counted, I could do this a bit to get to more accessible parts of the waterfront.

I waited outside the library for the shuttle, when a man in his 80s walked out of the library and asked me about my backpack.

"Is it safe?" he asked when I told him about the scope of my hike.

"I haven't had any problems," I said. "I think if you treat people with respect, they do the same. People are mostly good." This last part made me remember Ronnie, the kind fisherman I had met on the Detroit River.

He scowled and said, "Don't you believe that for a minute."

His name was Al. He had lived a rather circuitous life, bouncing around the world in the Merchant Marines, then serving in the Army during Korea, then becoming a building contractor. Al had built up his life several times only to lose everything, and then to rebuild again from scratch. There was a strength in the way he stood that spoke of his unbending will that had persisted into his eighth decade. When the shuttle had not shown up an hour past when it was supposed to, I told Al I'd better get moving.

"Where was the shuttle going to take you?"

"Up to the singing bridge," I told him.

"No problem!" he said, as he limped to his truck and flipped down the tailgate so I could stow my pack.

Al gave me a tour of the area along the way. We drove by his house, took back roads that paralleled the shoreline, saw Charity Island, and an old shed sitting out in the lake that used to be part of transporting gypsum from the mines to ships. Al pulled over at a turnout where I could get a better look at the shed. There were several circular pylons stepping out in the lake where a series of towers and cables were anchored to convey the gypsum from the mine to the shed. A historical marker explained that Douglass Houghton had discovered the deposits here in 1837 on one of his exploratory journeys around the state. Gypsum is still mined there today; it is the white stuff in drywall. A modern pipeline takes the product out to boats now. Gypsum was also used to improve farmland years ago. It was almost miraculous how sprinkling it onto land that was too acidic could correct the pH and make the land yield crops.

I thanked Al and tried to give him some money for gas. "Oh no," he said backing away and waving his hands. "Can't take that. I don't believe in God, but if he does exist I'd like him to note this as a nice thing I did."

From the singing bridge (so named because the wooden boards used to make a melodic humming when driven over – it is now paved, so it no longer sings, but the name stuck), I hiked the rest of the way to lovely Tawas City and East Tawas, following the Alabaster Bike Path.


## Walking on the edge of the bay

Since I was hiking with all my camping gear, I decided to stay two days in East Tawas. This would allow me to do a day hike, a loop out to Tawas Point to see the lighthouse and a park there, then go back to the same place for the night. I could do this day hike with a much lighter pack, maybe needing to carry only my water bottle and my walking pole if the weather looked good.

There was a significant difference between Tawas and the rest of the smaller towns sprinkled between it and Bay City. Tawas is close to Lake Huron and has developed its bay shore with parks and marinas. This, along with the natural beauty of the Tawas Point State Park (which boasts a historic lighthouse and several shipwrecks in the shallows there), draws tourists. Tourism brought money, and money brought development, jobs, and a relative prosperity that I hadn't seen elsewhere in the Saginaw Bay region of Michigan.

There were plenty of lodging options to choose from, and I found the lovely East Tawas Junction B&B to settle into for two nights.

The first day there, I hiked a ten-mile loop out to the tip of Tawas Point and back. The point is a little hook of a peninsula reaching south into the top of Saginaw Bay. Many birds stop here during their migratory journeys, and I saw orioles flitting around feeders that were decorated with sliced oranges just for them. The first lighthouse was built on the point in 1853, but over the course of the next twenty years, the point of sand grew longer by more than a mile. This made the first lighthouse useless to ships, so another was commissioned. That lighthouse still stands in the state park, a tall white tower aside a red-roofed keeper's house.

I walked the marked trail out to the point, then hiked back along the water's edge. It was a hot day, with white, cumulous clouds billowing overhead.

I returned to the B&B. I had been told there was a gathering of women who met monthly there for dinner. It was kind of a welcoming committee to the city that had gotten out of hand; the women kept meeting with no particular agenda other than to catch up with each other. Leigh, the owner of the place, told me I could chip in a few dollars and eat with the group if I wanted, that they would be happy to include me. So I got ready for the gathering that evening. It rained while I showered, but cleared off before the group arrived.

I enjoy the solitude of the hike. I like the time to think and observe, the time to feel a different pace of moving through the land. This was the pace at which man had moved until beasts were tamed and machines created to transport him. I traveled a pretty constant three miles per hour, and only slowed if the terrain became wild or uneven, or toward the end of a particularly long day. At this speed I became attuned to input from all of my senses; smells and sights and sounds sharpened. I became used to the quiet and isolation. Still, I was also looking forward to a break from this at the evening's gathering.

What the isolation of most of my days had taking from me, though, was the ability to easily screen out extra input – the kind one gets when trying to have one conversation while surrounded by several others. I hadn't realized this until I was in the middle of the group talking to a couple of the women, and the buzzing of many other nearby conversations started to freak me out.

I excused myself to go inside to get a long-sleeved shirt. I pulled my shirt out of my backpack, then sat next to the pack on the floor in my room for a moment and centered myself, then I rejoined the group, a bit more cautious, making sure to stay to the edges of the gathering. It was a lovely group of women from the community, and I had a great time getting to know them.


## Rainbows and muskrats

After a day's hike north from Tawas Point, I arrived in Oscoda, a city built on the banks of the Au Sable River. Virtually every river you come across in the Great Lakes region will have a past associated with lumbering, the shearing of the trees from the land. This was true of the many wide rivers I crossed over on my hike around Lake Michigan, and is quite true of the Au Sable that flows into Lake Huron. There is even a monument to the work of the lumbermen erected inland there a few miles upriver. There are places on the hilly riverbanks still scarred from the logs sliding down them to crash and splash into the river a century or more in the past.

I hiked downtown for dinner and found that the central road through the city had been removed and the roadbed excavated in places to a considerable depth – in places, ten feet down. Hills of sand and dirt punctuated the main thoroughfare, and heavy machinery was parked and idle after a day of tearing at the gap between buildings. There in the middle of this deserted scene was a man sweeping a metal detector back and forth on the newly turned earth. He had headphones on to better hear the beeping of the machine, so I watched him a moment until he noticed me. I waved a hand and he lifted one of the earphones away from his head.

"Are you finding anything good?" I asked.

"A couple Buffalo nickels," he said, "and one British coin probably from the late 1700s."

"Cool."

"These streets may never be exposed like this again."

"Good luck," I told him.

After dinner, a rainbow underscored a dark cloud in the distance. The slash of bright color in the sky, of light broken into crayon streaks, was beautiful. I passed an inland pond on the way that was covered in a thick layer of duckweed, the surface a bright green. Geese sat along the edges with their half-grown goslings, so I gave them a wide berth, but one extra-protective goose still postured and hissed at me.

"Yeah, yeah. Calm down." I told her, widening my path even more to get around them. I noticed a muskrat in the pond. He was floating there, his back smeared with duckweed, his little face held barely above the waterline. He was stuffing his face – literally stuffing his face – with the duckweed, shoveling it in as fast as he could using his two clawed front paws. I expected to hear a *nom, nom, nom* sound from him, like a sumo wrestler at a buffet table. He was the chubbiest muskrat I'd ever seen.


## The happiest house

My sister has good friends who have a summer home north of Oscoda, and they were going to be up there the weekend I was hiking through. I planned to take the weekend off! Les and her husband Ron were there along with Luann and Bill (who own the house) and their friends from Scotland, Glenis and Charlie.

Bill and Luann had nicknamed the house "The Happy House," and if that weekend was any indication of the times had there, it was perfectly named. During my visit, Les and Ron drove me over to the nearby Lumberman's Monument, and we hiked the 272 steps down to the river. It was on the way back up the 272 steps, as I was chatting away while Les and Ron were trying to catch their breath, that I realized how much this hike had whipped me back into shape.

The inscription on the base of the Lumberman's Monument reads:

"Erected to perpetuate the memory of the pioneer lumbermen of
Michigan through whose labors was made possible
the development of the prairie states."

The bronze statue atop the base is of three men representing the different
phases of lumbering. In the center stands a man called a timber cruiser, the
man who would scout the forests and decide which trees to harvest. He
holds a compass. The man on one side of him holds a saw and an ax, representing the felling phase of the operation. These men were called sawyers.
The third man represents the river rats, the men who would guide the logs
once they were floating on the river. He holds a peavey, a thick-handled
tool with a claw on the end to grab and turn and push logs.

This monument was erected in 1931. Archival photos from the 1930s
show the monument standing in a barren landscape, appropriately, with
just a few birch trees growing to one side of the sculpture. Today, replanted
pines tower over the site, barely hinting at what the area looked like before
these hard-working men arrived with their compass and tools to fell and
float the giant pines to the sawmills.

In the town of Harrisville, I went to the state park office and made a reser-
vation for a campsite in Negwegon State Park. This park of over 3,500 acres
is undeveloped and rather wild. From the lighthouse north of Harrisville,
I walked the shoreline, hoping to stay at the water's edge all the way to my
campsite.

This stretch of shoreline – from Oscoda north for many miles – was the
sandiest stretch I had encountered on Lake Huron so far. This part of the
hike reminded me of the other side of the state's mitten, that long, sandy
shoreline on Lake Michigan. What any given stretch of shoreline would be
like was determined by three main factors:

Was the shoreline sheltered (like in a bay)? Then the edge of the lake
would probably be shallow and vegetated, since wave action was calmed
and these growths had time to build up and thrive. Wetlands could form
over time and sediments deposited.

What geological layer was exposed at the shore, or was there a deposit
of glacial till there? If limestone was exposed, the shoreline would be rocky.
If it was slate or shale, the shoreline could look like it had been paved, or it

might be covered with tens of thousands of tumbled pieces of the fractured, flat rock, the edges worn smooth by the lake tossing the pieces around for decades. If it was sandstone and the wind and waves had time to wear it away, you might find stretches of sand, though any loose sand on the west side of the lake would be gradually blown out into the water and deposited on the east side due to the prevailing weather patterns over the Great Lakes region.

Are you on the windward or leeward edge of the lake? The prevailing movement of wind toward the east is why the western sides of the lakes (the windward side), in general, are not as sandy as the western sides (the leeward side).

After the fun weekend filled with people, the solitude of the hike was even more isolating. On my last hike, I was often transported by my brother, Phil, to the start of a segment of the hike, or back home after completing a chunk of it. On some remote segments, he even shadowed me in the car, dropping me off, then picking me up 15 or 20 miles away at the end of the day. I had to admit that I missed him on this hike.

I pulled my cell phone out of my backpack and saw that I had a signal, so I called him.

"'ello, Guv'nor!" Phil answered with a British accent.

"Ah . . . hello," I said.

"I told myself that the next time you called, I'd use a British accent," he explained.

"Well done," I laughed.

"How's the hike?" he asked.

"Great. Les and Ron and their friends were up here last weekend. That was a lot of fun."

"Nice."

"Yep. But I miss you. No one teases me about how bad I smell on the hot days."

"I miss that, too. Well, not that, specifically – but being part of it all."

"How does your schedule look? Can you get away and come up here for a few days?" We chatted a bit more. Phil said he'd try to carve time out of his schedule to come north.

## Predator and prey

When I ended up in a bog as I neared Negwegon State Park, I backtracked, walked the road for a bit, then cut onto the trails looping through the park.

I found the artesian well that had been designated as a water source in the park. There was a slab of cement over the tapped well and a large, bent pipe splashed water on the cement. It was constantly flowing, so a small wetland thrived nearby.

The day was warm, so I took my pack off and leaned it against a nearby tree where it wouldn't get wet. Then, I took my glasses off and plunged my head under the cold water brought up from the depths of the earth. The chill of it took my breath away. I splashed more on my face, then filled my water bottles, reunited with my pack, and hiked the short distance to the beach.

This park has a sandy, curved beach. I took off my boots and socks and walked out into the water. Since the days had been so warm and this area was so shallow and protected, the water had heated up to about 70 degrees. After enjoying the warm water on my feet, I geared up again and began hiking the shoreline to my campsite, just a mile north. Soon I was tangled in reeds and sinking into a clay deposit, so I hiked back to the beach, cut inland, and hiked the wide trail. Where the trail went over wetlands, a wooden boardwalk had been installed. The hike was easy, as the trail passed through dense and varied forests.

Negwegon was a chief of a Chippewa tribal group that had lived in this area in the 1700s. This park used to be called Alpena State Park, but a local woman, Hazlet Kramer, was an advocate for the Native Americans and pushed to have the name changed to honor this chief. Since this land remained undeveloped and wild, I thought it fitting to connect it to the Native Americans, compared to a park that might have been filled with campers and cars, overrun with people.

There are only four camping sites in the park, all situated on the shoreline. I set up camp, pulling essentials out of my backpack, stringing my hammock tent between two trees, set out my cooking gear and dehydrated food, and gathered wood for a fire. The ranger had told me I'd probably be the only one staying the night in the park, that all the other sites were open.

As I ate my rehydrated dinner, I looked out on the lake. Gulls circled overhead, white against the wispy, cirrus clouds. Red-winged blackbirds warned the gulls to stay away from their nest in the cattails near the shore.

At a little after 6 p.m., I had eaten, cleaned up, strung my food bag up the bear pole, and was ready to light the campfire. Actually, I was ready to go to sleep, but knew that it was too early and I'd probably wake up in the middle of the night, ready to start the next day.

There were very few mosquitoes. Mayflies multiplied as the shadows lengthened; they flew around in a loose, wayward swarm. I saw a few ants patrolling the area, and large spiders sitting in their webs, spanning some of the gaps between grasses and branches.

An hour later, I put another small log on the fire and wondered if it was bedtime yet. The only manmade sound I heard was the far-off whistle from a passing train.

Around 8 p.m., I spread the coals around the fire ring, doused them thoroughly with water, then wiggled into my hammock tent. I had left the rain fly off since there were no clouds to bring rain and the wind had calmed. I got comfortable on top of my sleeping bag and looked up through the fine mesh that is the only thing between the sky and me. The gulls – about 30 of them – circled lower, almost touching the tops of the short trees. I wondered if they were eating the swarm of mayflies they were gliding through. I wrote in my notebook for a bit, then snuggled into my sleeping bag and watched the blue fade from the sky and the green drain from the leaves as the sun set.

The sky over the lake turned bright yellow, streaked with orange, then mellowed to a burgundy wine splash in the clouds and along the horizon. With the tilt of the earth's axis and the curve of my shoreline, I was able to watch the sun set into the lake to the northwest. In the morning, that same sun would pop out of the lake to the southeast.

In the middle of the night, I awoke to the sound of something moving between me and the lake. There was a soft light in the black leaves above me, and when I put my glasses on, I saw distinct stars shining in the gaps between the leaves.

An animal cried out, struggled, thrashed about. It cried again, softer, almost pleading. Then, silence. The predator/prey drama was played out about 30 feet from me.

Owl vs. squirrel? The screaming was too loud for a squirrel. Maybe an ermine?

Bobcat vs. raccoon? It was too dark to see, and the sounds too universal to identify. I just knew that the prey fought for its life and lost. It was primal and brutal. It made me break out in a cold sweat and shiver in my warm sleeping bag.

## Alpena onward

After breaking camp the next morning, I hiked the back roads – sandy, narrow, and rugged lanes – toward the town of Ossineke (pronounced *Oz-NEEK)*. There was a small restaurant where the little lane I was walking joined up with US 23, a perfect place to get out of the heat for a bit. I took a table on the edge of the room since I was a bit grungy after camping. The place was bustling with locals who knew the waitresses by name, along with a few summer people. At one round table, three men and one woman sat, all in their late 60s or early 70s, and there was a resemblance between them. After I had paid for my BLT and stood to get ready to hoist my pack back onto its place on my back, one of the men asked, "Are you on a trek?"

"Yes," I said, "A thousand miles!"

I pulled out my card and stepped over to their table.

We chatted a bit, and the woman said, "These are my brothers. We meet up once a week for lunch."

I smiled, remembering how I was missing my own brother, Phil. "So, you get together to tease each other once a week?" We all laughed.

When she found out that I was keeping to the shoreline all the way to Mackinaw City, the woman, Rosalie, offered to let me stay with her. She lived north of the 40-Mile Point Lighthouse, just north of Rogers City. She wrote her name and contact information in neat printing and handed me the piece of paper. I often had strangers make this kind offer, but had never taken anyone up on it. Part of my adventure was that I was to be self-reliant, finding my way, camping here and there. I put the paper inside a plastic bag, though, in case I changed my mind.

I hiked along US 23 into the small town of Ossineke and came across another monument to the lumbermen. There are concrete statues along the road of Paul Bunyan and Babe, his blue ox. Paul is about 25 feet tall and Babe about 10 feet at the tip of his horns. I snapped some photos using the timer function on my camera, so I could run over to lean on the handle of Paul Bunyan's ax. Then, another shot of me reaching up to touch Babe's blue nose.

I stayed at a place on the lakeshore in Ossineke. At night, I could look up Thunder Bay to the shoreline of the city of Alpena. The remarkable feature of the city at night is that the Lafarge cement plant lights up like a glowing display every night. The lights reflected on the bay, doubling the effect, like stars had fallen into the water and kept shining.

The next day, I hiked north along the sandy shoreline for miles until I neared Squaw Bay. There, I began to see scattered pieces of shale and soon I was walking on a thick layer of broken shale. This is the same shale formation that is exposed on the shoreline of Lake Michigan across the state at this same latitude.

An elderly man was on his beach raking up the algae that waves had deposited thickly on the edge of the water. I chatted with him and he told me that he liked to use the algae to fertilize his garden, but it was too much work to haul it there now, so he gathers and buries it so it wouldn't rot and smell in the heat.

"I've noticed some oily residue coming out of the groundwater here," I said. "Has it always been like that?"

"We've owned this place for 23 years," he said, "and the groundwater has always been bad here. We've gone through many filtration systems trying to get it good enough to just shower with. We used to bring in bottled water to drink and cook with." He pointed to the shale in the water. "Petroleum and natural gas is in pockets within these rock deposits, and it leaches out with the groundwater. They finally brought the city water out this way for us to hook into."

"Alpena gets its water from out in the lake, correct?"

He nodded. "They have the same trouble with well water all along the bay, so the city pulls from Lake Huron and cleans it up."

"Back by Harrisville, I saw large oil slicks on the streams feeding into the lake."

He nodded. "Yep. It's all under the state."

The Nature Conservancy has purchased and protected much of Squaw Bay – the small, scooped bay within Thunder Bay south of Alpena – and the wetlands there were alive with mussels and fish, turtles and frogs and water-fowl. A giant catfish cruised the shallows, then turned and disappeared into the water plants. I had to hike down the embankment to get to the water, and would learn that the bay here used to be at the level of the road, about 10 feet higher than it is presently. One consequence of the lake levels retreating is that wetlands can become stranded, cut off from the lake. This severing is not healthy for the lakes because wetlands are vital places for fish to spawn; they also serve as a place where water is naturally filtered before joining the larger body of water. If the isolated wetland does not have its own source of water, it may even dry up completely. While Squaw Bay still looked healthy, it was certainly diminished from what it once was.

## Employee relations built on blocks of concrete

I hiked the city of Alpena around the curve of Thunder Bay. There are several parks along the bay there with paved paths that I could stroll along. Each successive park gave an even more stunning view of the Lafarge concrete plant – one of the largest concrete plants in the world – that has occupied a tract of land on the edge of the bay since 1908. Today, the plant produces 2.5 million tons of cement each year. The concrete industry has been the economic foundation of Alpena for the last century. The Besser Company has also thrived there for over a century. It was here that Jessie Besser patented and then continued his entire life to improve machines to produce concrete blocks.

Any company that has survived that long has worked through some major events: two world wars, the depression, and unionization of workers (to name a few). When unionization led to strikes and strife between workers and management, Besser established clubs for its workers and management to mingle together after work, to erase the division between the two groups and keep everyone friendly. After WWII, they established a men's chorus. I saw an old black-and-white photo of the Besser Male Chorus from decades ago. The company had hired a professional director to lead the group. In the photo, he stands in the center in his white tuxedo with a dark boutonniere. On risers behind him are fifty men in black tuxes with white carnations on their lapels. It's a snazzy group of men, transformed from the dusty work clothes worn while cranking out concrete blocks. This group won many awards over the years and performed at such august events as the inauguration of Governor George W. Romney (Mitt's father) and the groundbreaking ceremony for the beginning of construction on the Mackinac Bridge.

From Alpena, I planned to hike to Michigan's newest state recreation area that includes the 300-acre, old Rockport limestone mine. It was from here that the huge limestone slabs were carved to support the Mackinac Bridge. I planned to camp at the park for one night, then hike north to Presque Isle the following day.

As I hiked north out of Alpena, I remembered a scientific paper I had read about a time when the Great Lakes were quite young (~8,000 years ago). Lake Huron was much more shallow than it is today, and there was a land bridge that crossed the lake. If exposed today, the land bridge would allow you to walk east from Alpena over to Point Clark in Ontario on dry land. This feature is now submerged in Lake Huron.

You may wonder why scientists are so interested in this bridge, using high-resolution bathometry and 3-D surface modeling to study it. The answer is that the submerged land bridge holds evidence of early man that has been preserved underwater for thousands of years. Scientists have discovered rocks arranged in patterns to drive animals being hunted. They've documented marker rocks along the bridge at certain intervals, and possible remains of ancient dwellings. The paper notes, unfortunately, that invasive mussels and algae are progressively obscuring the topography of the site.

## Fancy fish lures

There are two large inland lakes between Alpena and Presque Isle: Long Lake and Grand Lake. Along with Lake Huron, these offer many opportunities for anglers to toss in a line and catch a fish or two. I stopped in at a bait shop near the edge of Long Lake and bought a cold drink. The shop was owned and operated by a father-daughter team, and since their store was air-conditioned and they were willing to chat, I sat down a while to talk lures and fish and the Great Lakes with Budd and Lorie.

It turned out that they not only sold fishing gear, but Lorie designed her own line of lures (Lorie Rigs) that were on display in the shop, along with many photos of the fish lured by the lures.

"A guy once showed me this special rig he had bought somewhere," Lorie said. "I took one look at it and thought, 'I can do better than that'!" She showed me a couple of her fancy rigs.

"Lots of anglers swear by these lures and catch everything from perch to walleye and bass on them."

Now, I confess I'm a drown-the-worm angler when I fish. These rigs were clearly out of my league.

"So the fishery is good here?" I asked.

"Lake Huron has been spotty at best lately, but the inland lakes – Long Lake and Grand Lake – are fantastic," Budd said.

"Have you noticed a change in the level of Lake Huron?" I asked.

"Sure," Budd said. "If you go out to the dock at Rockport –"

"That's where I'm heading today," I said.

"There's a huge pier there, at least what's left of it. The wood pilings used to be far under water, but they're all exposed now. The water level is down about ten feet from when the quarry was active."

They told me an ice-fishing story of some guys fishing one winter out in the harbor there. They placed their tip-ups out on the ice (they tip up to give a visible signal when a fish takes the bait). To their dismay, at some point when they check, they realized their tip-ups had completely disappeared. They were just gone.

"The lake waves were rolling underneath the ice. They could barely feel it, but the swells were strong enough to open a crack in the ice sheet, swallow their gear, then close back up."

I got up and shouldered my pack. "You've got to respect the power of the big lakes," I said, heading for the door. They nodded and wished me well on my journey.

I had spoken to scientists at the Great Lakes Science Center in Ann Arbor about the declining fishery – especially salmon – in Lake Huron. One researcher, Dr. Madenjian, explained that anytime prior to 1995, Lake Huron's population of salmon was 90% hatchery fish and only 10% wild. By the year 2000, the proportions had flipped. Now, 90% were wild (offspring spawned in the wild) and only 10% hatchery-born. Something had happened – scientists still aren't sure what it was – so that the spawning of the salmon was now incredibly successful.

I had seen many salmon pulled from the lakes, but wasn't sure how you could tell a hatchery fish from a wild one. Dr. Madenjian told me that they clip the fin of the hatchery fish to mark them.

"Lake Huron has always had fewer alewives than Lake Michigan," Dr. Madenjian explained, "so these millions of new salmon just ate them up."

"I've read reports that many of the salmon have moved over to Lake Michigan," I said.

He nodded. "These fish are used to hunting in the Pacific Ocean, so moving through the Straits of Mackinac in search of prey would be nothing to them. Nothing. If you're interested in the native fish in the lakes, this salmon migration to the west has been good for the trout here. They've come back a bit in Lake Huron since the salmon have declined."

The Great Lakes Science Center does work to understand the complex interactions in the ecosystem of the lakes. When I asked Dr. Bunnell about the big picture, he was optimistic. "When you look at the health of the lakes compared to the 1960s and '70s," he said, "it's a good time for the lakes."

When we discussed the biggest threats to these inland seas, he agreed with my assessment that the greatest dangers lay with the increasing populations of invasive species – the mussels, especially – and a larger quantity of algae blooming as the lakes get incrementally warmer.

## Great bear country

It took a couple of hours to hike to the Rockport dock from the bait shop. The far end of the wide pier had been mostly swept away by waves. Now, only the wooden pilings poked up between the end of the surviving pier and a far-off, metal-encircled concrete support. There were a few people in the park, some swimming, some tossing fishing lines in the water. The landscape looked altered from its natural state. Tailings from the mine were piled in mini-mountains near the shoreline. A few scrubby bushes had taken hold on the mounds and were struggling to grow. Rusted and twisted metal pieces were scattered about, the remnants of old mining equipment.

I unbuckled my pack and let it rest against a tree while I hiked a loop around the area, trying to find the actual quarry. An old road led me right to it. The land had been torn up decades ago to liberate the stone used to build the bridge spanning the straits. There were many fossils in the area, ancient corals that spoke of a time when this land was covered in a shallow, salty sea. I crossed paths with a baby groundhog. We stopped to study each other. I'd never seen a baby groundhog before, and it's likely I was the first human he had ever seen, so it was quite a meeting.

I hiked back to my pack, noticing a number of "No Camping" and "Area Under Video Surveillance" signs. Along with the barren landscape of the mine, these made me decide to hike through the park and head on to

Presque Isle for the night instead of camping illegally there. It would add a long extra hike to the long day I had already put in, but the old mining road stayed pretty close to the lake and I was less than comfortable with the idea of video surveillance in the area. I took off at a quick pace and worked my way through the wilderness.

The sun was beginning to go down and the woods got thicker as I hiked. It started to look like really good bear country. I heard coyote yipping in the woods and a murder of ravens squawking like they owned the place. I started singing out loud to alert any larger carnivores lurking about to my presence. One was my impression of Ethel Merman singing "There's No Business Like Show Business." I even added some jazz hands along the way.

I was pretty sure no self-respecting bear would be able to eat me after that.

Another song I often sang was a two-part opera I made up. In the lowest voice I could manage, I'd sing, "Don't eat me, I don't taste good, you think that I would, but I don't!" That would be followed by my highest voice singing, "Actually, I am delicious, but I won't tell that to you!" I'd switch back and forth between the parts, arguing with myself in two voices. Somehow, I figured this would not only entertain and alert the top of the food chain, but would also make them think there was possibly more than one of me. I'm not sure how convinced they were, but hey, I emerged without getting any invitations to be dinner!

The sun had set by the time I got to Presque Isle. There was still a glow in the western sky, but the shadows were diffuse. Owls were beginning to awaken in the forest, calling out. I arrived at the lodge there that was nearly a century old and checked in. The upstairs floors sloped and tilted, guiding me to my room. I dropped my pack, unlaced my boots, and collapsed into bed shortly after opening the windows to let in the night air.

In the morning, I awakened to loons calling to each other on Grand Lake.

Presque Isle is French for "almost island." The French would use this to designate a peninsular landform. While they may have used this as a general term, the name actually stuck to many places. Presque Isle, Michigan, north of Alpena is not even the only Presque Isle in Michigan. There is another one in the Upper Peninsula. I would also hike by one later on the Canadian side of Lake Ontario, and there's one in eastern Lake Erie.

It probably wasn't a problem a couple of hundred years ago when people didn't travel enough to get confused between places that were hundreds of miles apart, but as I researched these areas online, I had to double-check that the B&B or park I was researching was in the part of the Great Lakes that I was hiking and not an entirely different lake or state or even another country.

Presque Isle is off the beaten track in Michigan. You wouldn't drive through it to get from one place to another. You'd have to make plans to go there, to swing wide to the east, to get on the other side of Grand Lake. And that is part of the charm of the area: it is not overrun and the loons still call to each other in the morning.

It is here that Lake Huron's shoreline curves to the northwest, heading to the tip of Michigan's mitten, to Mackinaw City.


## Lightning rod

There are only two small towns between Presque Isle and Mackinaw City at the tip of Michigan's mitten: Rogers City and Cheboygan. With a long, rugged stretch before I would reach Rogers City, I planned to camp one night on the shores of Lake Huron. When I left the Presque Isle lodge, I hiked the rugged, rocky shore with the Presque Isle lighthouse in sight across North Bay, making my way into Thompson's Harbor State Park. Along a curve of shore there, the rocks slowly gave way to a sandy beach.

Dragonflies patrolled the area in squadrons, and killdeer cried out as I neared their nest. I took a break on the small dunes, thankful to see sand again. Storm clouds were gathering, but the weather people had promised they would stay well to the north of me.

I explored the park a bit, hiking the shoreline where I could, then taking to the trails when it got too marshy to stay at the water's edge. As I neared the northern end of the park, lightning split the sky. Counting the seconds between strikes, I determined that the storm was only eight miles off, and the billowing, gray clouds were heading my way.

I moved faster, trying to recall all I had learned about handling yourself in a lightning storm in survival guides or on adventure documentaries on TV. The only thing that sprang to mind was an episode of *The Waltons* where Jim Bob is in the woods with Mama and a storm catches them. Jim Bob remembers all the lessons Grandpa told him about not going into a hollow tree "Those are called 'Widow-makers,' Mama, we don't want to shelter there." Remembering his Grandpa's folksy lessons, Jim Bob kept them safe through the storm. I looked down at my aluminum walking pole and thought, *What about walking with a metal stick, Jim Bob? What did Grandpa say about that?*

The next lightning strike hit three miles away. I felt the thunder rumble in my chest. When the sprinkle of rain turned to sheets of water, I decided I needed some kind of shelter and that it might be best to stash my metal walking pole away from me. On the rugged two-track through the woods, I came upon a truck parked at a trailhead. The cab was empty, which meant that others were out in the storm, too.

Water dripped off my rain gear, so I didn't even try the cab doors to see if they were unlocked. Peeking inside, I saw that the tidy cab had a clean blanket covering the seat, and a mystery novel sat in the middle alongside a small GPS unit. My first impression is that the owner was a nice person, one who possibly traveled with a dog.

The bed of the truck was protected with a snapped-down vinyl cover. I knew from my brother-in-law's truck that unsnapping it was unwise as it would be difficult to re-snap. I tried the tailgate, hoping to slide under the cover out of the rain and wait out the storm. But it was locked, so I put my pack and pole a distance away from the truck underneath a short tree. I draped a trash bag over the pack to keep the rain from soaking the interior. Then I returned to the vehicle and stepped up on the truck bed, clinging to the tailgate and balancing there on the back bumper.

Even if lightning struck nearby, the truck's tires would insulate me from the electric jolt.

The rain pounded down so thickly that it was difficult to see, but I could tell the lightning strikes were more frequent because the thunder was almost constant, one rolling wave of sound overtaking another. I cursed the weather forecasters as I perched there, hunching over, water streaming off my hood and into the tall grass around the truck.

When the rain eventually let up, I decided to try to take a photo of myself. I looked at it and decided that I looked too frightened in the photo. I tried to relax and take another, but I still look freaked out. I tried a goofy grin for the third photo, but ended up looking deranged, so I gave up and put the camera away.

The rain still came down, with occasional peals of thunder and flashes of lightning, when I saw a man and his beagle making their way toward me from the lakeshore. I stayed perched on the back of the truck until they drew near, then hopped off and introduced myself.

"I rode out the lightning on the back of your truck. I hope you don't mind," I said.

The storm seemed to have mostly passed over now.

"That's fine," he nodded and his dog checked me out before jumping up into the cab. The man looked up at the sky. "I usually don't worry about lightning as long as there are things around that are taller than me." He unlocked the tailgate and tossed his wooden walking stick inside with the tools and lumber there.

"I have that aluminum walking pole," I explained, pointing to my lightning rod.

He nodded. "That might be a problem." He pulled a large stone from his pocket. "Got this for the wife. She collects pudding stones."

I admired the palm-sized reddish stone embedded with smaller, multi-colored stones. "That's a pretty one."

"Sorry the truck wasn't unlocked for you."

"Oh, I wouldn't have gone in the cab anyway. Not soaked like this. But thanks." I shook his hand and then went over to my pack. I shook out, folded, and tucked the trash bag back in the pack and shouldered it. Then, I picked up my lightning rod and waved to the kind man and his dog and headed northwest again.

I figured that the weather people had been wrong about that line of storms, but they wouldn't be wrong about the clear night, right? I'd be camping in a perfectly clear night, for sure, right?

I hiked through the woods for many more miles. The rain had refreshed everything. The greens were sharper, and the woods smelled piney and like stirred earth. Indian paintbrush bloomed and blazed along the trail, along with wild, bright orange lilies. Raindrops beaded on their wide petals.

Land snails moved out onto the path, leaving slimy trails. A centipede over two inches long cruised among the rocks. Up close I could see that each of its black segments was outlined in brownish burgundy, giving it a snazzy, striped exoskeleton.

Two bald eagles soared over the bay. One was mature with a bright white head, the other still a juvenile, its head still brown. At one point, I walked along the edge of a beaver dam. These hydro-engineers had dammed a stream, creating a lush wetland behind the thick wall of sticks and dirt. A slow trickle of water exited from around and under the dam, so shallow that I could splash my way through it.

I finally found a stretch of rocky beach skirted with trees, and decided it was a good place to stop for the night. I set up camp and boiled some water. As I ate my rehydrated stew, I noticed clouds gathering again – thunderheads, those mountainous clouds that promise to hold more rain than you thought possible – and I cursed the weather people. All of them.

As I looked out on the lake, I noticed a creature on one of the large rocks in the shallows near shore. I figured a brown bird had landed there, but it didn't move like a bird. It was sinewy and it curled around itself, smoothing the fur on its back: a river otter. He poured himself off the rock and slipped into the water, glided around a bit, then dove. I watched him dive and resurface repeatedly as the light faded from the sky.

I secured my food bag up a tree, then checked my hammock tent and rain fly. The hammock has an underlayer separate from the hammock, a rubberized second layer that was designed to use in cooler weather with a pad slipped in between the two layers. I had left it on for this trip, figuring it was a good space to store gear I might need but didn't want inside with me. This night, I thought I might need access to my raincoat, so I stuffed it underneath the hammock and on top of the rubberized layer. My sleeping bag, extra clothes in a waterproof bag, my knife, and my flashlight all got stowed inside the hammock.

I heard thunder in the distance, so I also took my iPad out of my backpack and placed it inside the hammock. I figured I might want to have a distraction to take my mind off of the impending storm.

## A most refreshing drink of water

Sure I had everything I needed from my pack, I slipped a trash bag over it, then hung it on a tree branch so it would be up off the ground.

As it began to sprinkle, I slithered into my hammock through the slit in the bottom. The rain steadily increased. The water-drops gathered and streamed off the fly, then the rain really picked up, and sheets of water cascaded off the edge. I congratulated myself on having such a well-designed shelter that lifted me off the ground and kept me safe and dry.

The thunder and lightning came with shorter pauses, and I pulled my iPad out of its neoprene sleeve. Firing it up, I pulled up an article on whales. I wanted to take my mind off the storm, to let it pass without counting the gap between every lightning strike and thunder to determine how close the bolts were getting to me, suspended between two trees in the wet wilderness. I always chose short trees to hang my hammock tent, but it was still unnerving to have lightning cracking overhead so close that I could feel the charge in the air.

The article was engaging, and soon I was following the whales out in the ocean, riding on a boat, watching them surface and blow as they travel in a pod. *Wow, this is really well written,* I thought, *I actually feel like I'm floating on the water! Ha ha!*

I figured it must be the rocking motion of the hammock as the storm blew the trees I was suspended between, but then I placed my hand underneath my sleeping bag and realized that I was sitting in a pool of water. I strained to see the lake through the bug mesh. When the lightning flashed, I confirmed that it is still well away from me; the lake had not risen up to swallow me. So where was this water coming from? I shifted from side-to-side and felt a pool of water sloshing underneath me: the rubberized under-hammock was filling with water!

I quickly slid the iPad back into its neoprene sleeve and shoved it up near the elevated end of the tent, then I grabbed my knife and wiggled my way out and into the storm. The trees that the hammock is strung between had sagged with the weight of me and all the water. Getting out of a hammock tent is never graceful, but in this saggy, soggy state it was like being birthed. I pushed out, legs first, and then thrashed and wiggled my way through the opening and fell with a splash of water onto the rocks below. The end of my sleeping bag poked through the opening like a soggy, trailing placenta.

I unfolded the biggest blade on my knife and studied the rubberized layer. It bulged with gallons of water – gallons! – a mini-lake rising up beneath the hammock tent. It seemed that when I stored my raincoat, the back edge of this layer poked out underneath the fly to catch the water streaming off in buckets. I slashed at the point where this water-filled layer connected to the support ropes until it fell away. The mini-lake it held cascaded over my bare feet and between the rocks. I shook out my soaked raincoat and tossed it over a branch. Since my clothes were soaked, I strip off my shirt and pants and hang them, too. Then I hunched there in my underwear under the rain fly to think about what to do next.

Lightning split the sky over the lake, illuminating it for brief seconds: the waves, the streams of water running between and over the rocks to meet the lake. Lightning struck again, closer; the crash of thunder was immediate.

"Enough already!" I yelled to the sky.

I remembered a story about the naturalist, John Muir, and how he once tied himself to the top of a tall tree during a storm in order to feel how the tree felt in the wind and rain. In that moment, with lightning followed immediately by thunder so loud and close that it reverberated inside my ribcage, I was sure that Mr. Muir did not do this in a *thunder* storm. If not for the threat of being struck by lightning, I probably would have put on my boots and danced on the rocky beach in my underwear, in the warm rain, joining Mr. Muir in his revelry.

Crouching there, I realized that even though I am surrounded by water and soaking wet, I am incredibly thirsty. I stood and let the rain hit my face, opening my mouth to catch the fat droplets. This method would take all night. I looked at the rain fly and noticed a depression where water had gathered. Leaning over, I stuck my lips into the little pool and sucked it dry. This was the coolest, most refreshing drink of water I have ever experienced. The depression refilled; I drank the pure, cold water over and over again.

Then, with no other options, I twisted the water out of the end of my sleeping bag, and wiggled back in the hammock tent on top of it. Inside, I realized that my iPad case had slid down into the pool of water. I pulled my shammy towel out of my dry bag and toweled myself off, then wrapped the towel around the iPad hoping to save it. I stuck the iPad, swaddled in its case, back into the upper corner of the hammock and thrashed around, putting on some dry clothes pulled from the waterproof bag. I jammed the wet half of my sleeping bag into a garbage bag and then placed it on top of me. I put a pair of dry socks on my hands. It was past midnight by the time I got as settled in again as was possible given the circumstances. I tried to get some rest . . . damp, cool, and not in the best mood.

I dozed on and off until the sun lifted out of the lake several short hours later, blazing the horizon with a band of orange. Truth be told, I prefer my sun to *set* on the lake, but that day I welcomed its morning light and warmth. I wanted to get back to civilization, to shower, to wash my clothes, and to hunt down those damn weather people.

And to answer your question: No, iPads do not recover from being dunked in water.

At least mine didn't.


## Purple martins and an evil king

I had made arrangements with a friend of a friend to stay at the Purple Martin B&B in Rogers City. Details of the place had been sketchy, but intriguing: an old building – actually a defunct commercial facility that used to do laundry for the lake freighters – was being converted into a B&B/community center/non-profit organization. Its income would go to support work with foster kids in Rogers City. A laundry/B&B/community center/foster-kids place was difficult to picture. The only photos I had seen online in advance were from a volunteer workday, with students from Central Michigan University who had travelled up to the place to help with the renovations. That was the year prior to my hike, so I assumed that the establishment was complete and open for business. Turns out, it was still undergoing its transformation. But one bedroom was set up and available for my stay.

I met two women at the building, Marilou and Ruth. I was exhausted from the night before, spent swimming in a hammock, and was still a little clammy. The women swirled around me, showing me to my room, pointing out the shower in the kitchen, then fighting over who got to do my laundry. I borrowed some rice from one of them. I had heard that the grains could help dry out wet electronic devices, so I tossed the rice into a bag with my also-still-clammy iPad and cell phone. Then, I took a long shower and got back into dry clothes in time to go out to eat with my two new friends. The owner of the place, Cindy, called to make sure I had arrived. My phone was also little wet and wonky, but I spoke to her a bit, then tossed the phone back into the bag of rice.

The ladies took me on a driving tour of the city as another line of thunderstorms bore down on us. Branches broke off trees and scooted across the two inches of water blowing in ripples across the streets.

"This weather was supposed to stay north of us," Ruth said, looking up at the green-gray sky.

*Tell me about it,* I thought.

Rogers City has a fascinating history tied to the lumber industry, the lake, and the limestone. The early history of the town is so fantastical it seems borrowed from a daytime soap opera. The main figure was Albert Molitor who was (. . . wait for it . . .) the illegitimate son of the king of Wurtemberg (a kingdom in what is now Germany). Molitor was given a decent position in the Wurtembergian War Department, but was arrested after attempting to sell plans of the fortress of Uhlan to the French (something that was apparently frowned upon). He was ordered to leave the country, so he came to America during the Civil War. He served in the war and afterward partnered with William E. Rogers to found Rogers City around 1870.

Molitor ruled the place like an evil king. Historic accounts state that he ran the company town brutally, overcharging at the company store, taxing people and keeping the money for himself, positioning himself in various government offices, and choosing the civil servants to serve under him as his lackeys. The stories I heard from people living in Rogers City today went even further: people said that he chose women and young girls from the families and used these women as his personal servants and bedmates.

The historical record is clear, though, on what happened to Molitor: the townspeople rose up and murdered him. Molitor was such a horrible man that the crime went unprosecuted for twenty years and only came to trial when one of the participants confessed decades later. Several men were given life in prison for the crime, but were pardoned by the governor after serving a little over three years.

Current-day Rogers City, in contrast, is so lovely and welcoming that its past seems almost unbelievable. People in the town went out of their way to greet me warmly. Ruth and Marilou taxied me to the office of the town newspaper to be interviewed, I got a lovely tour of the town and limestone mine, and a member of the City Council even stopped by to meet me!

"Can I do anything for you?" Councilwoman Debbie asked me. We sat together on the upper deck of the Purple Martin B&B, looking out on Lake Huron and watching the purple martins swoop and dive and land on birdhouses nearby. "Can I get you anything?"

"No," I said. "Thanks, though. Everyone here has been so nice and helpful."

She looked off at the lake. "We don't see people from the outside much."

I cracked up, but stopped laughing when she didn't smile.

"Really. We don't," she said.

## Limestone!

Oh, the limestone mine! The owner of the B&B's boyfriend, Larry, works there, and he took me on a tour before sunset. The scale of the mine dwarfed the dump trucks that were making perpetual loops in the distance through the barren rockscape. They looked like toys when I first saw them, but when we got closer, I realized that their tires were around ten feet tall and the driver had to climb a long ladder running up alongside the radiator to reach the cab.

"Those trucks carry over 200 tons in each load. This mine is the largest open-pit limestone mine in the world," Larry told me. "We've pulled limestone out for 100 years, and they estimate there is another 100 years worth of limestone still here."

In fact, I had spied banners hanging around Rogers City announcing the 100th anniversary of the Calcite Mine.

We watched the dump trucks back up to a structure where the limestone was dumped to be processed. "The load goes in there," Larry said, "then it's transported to the top of that building and sorted by size on the way down through different-sized grates. Different-sized pieces are used for different things."

I'd read a little about it in advance. "I know it's used in the production of steel and cement and even in getting sugar from sugar beets. Anything else?"

"Dow Chemical sends a boat here regularly. They use it in their production of certain chemicals. They are pretty particular about the chemical composition of their limestone."

"Ruth told me she used to work in the lab here to test each load."

Larry nodded.

"She also told me she worked security here, and that that part of the operation was run by the Pinkertons! I didn't know they were still around!"

"Yep."

We watched the sorted limestone pour off the end of the conveyor arms into tall piles, then drove by the dock where a massive freighter was tied to accept a load of limestone.

"It takes 8 to 12 hours to load each ship," Larry told me.

As we drove away from the mine, the red-orange globe of the sun was setting behind the tree line, smearing the sky with color.

## Lady of the Flies

The next day I ate my breakfast on the patio of the B&B and discovered a small, yellow bird sitting on the ground there. It was alive, but looked like it had been roughed up a bit. I brought out some water and wet its beak. At first I thought it was a finch, but the beak was too pointy, and it had red streaks on its breast and a little orange on its head. Turns out it was a yellow warbler. The little guy was probably blown down in the storm the previous day.

"The weather people said the storms would stay north of us," I told him, so the little guy would know the depths of that betrayal. He shook his head and I knew I had an ally in my intended campaign against the deceitful weather people. I left a capful of water for him, and was happy to see he was hopping around by the time I had gone inside to stuff my belongings back into my pack and set out for the lakeshore again.

The forecast predicted it would warm into the 90s, so I knew I couldn't hike my normal fifteen-mile day. I called Rosalie whom I had met and chatted with in the diner in Ossineke where she was having lunch with her brothers. I asked if she might allow me to stay the night since she was within my 10-mile limit for the hot day. She welcomed me to do just that.

Any day that got near or above 80 degrees was problematic for me, especially when I was carrying my heavy pack, made even heavier with the addition of my camping gear for this month's hike. I tend to not sweat enough to keep cool, so I had to resort to wetting a bandana and tying it around my neck, or even wetting a long-sleeved shirt and wearing it until it dried, then wetting it again. I used ice when it was available, rolling it up in a bandana and tying that around my neck. That worked well until it all melted.

On this day, I began hiking in shorts and short-sleeved shirt, but when I got to the lakeshore, stable flies swarmed me. Now, when I say "swarmed," you may imagine a cloud of ten or so flies, maybe twenty. I've seen them in this quantity along the lakeshore at times, and it's plenty pesky. But on this day there were hundreds dancing around me, each trying to land so it could bite a chunk from me. Literally hundreds.

Stable flies look like small house flies, but they bite. And it hurts. They tend to bite exposed ankles and legs or neck, and today they were even trying to get me through my thick socks (which were impregnated with bug repellent). I zipped on my pant legs and kept walking. They swarmed my arms, so I put on a thin long-sleeved shirt and kept walking, as briskly as I could manage with my heavy pack in the soft sand. They began biting my hands, so I sprayed the back of my hands with bug repellent. This only worked as long as the repellent was wet, when it dried they resumed their attempts to bite. A few worked their way under the collar of my shirt, so I covered my head with my bandana and tied it under my chin.

Oh, what a fashion statement I was making!

As I walked, more flies joined the party. I could look down at my pant legs and count over 100 flies attached there, sitting and waiting their chance to strike. The winter had been mild, which probably contributed to the large population of flies this summer. That, and the extra-hot weather may have brought them all out at once. The ones attached to my pants seemed to be lulled by my walking; I was able to swat large groupings and watch up to twenty of them fall off dead from the blow. This was oddly satisfying, but the flies circling me immediately took the places of their dead comrades.

## The halfway point

As I approached the 40-Mile Point Lighthouse, I realized that I had reached the halfway point of my adventure: 500 miles! I took a moment to record some video. In it, I am red-faced and wrapped up, the sky is bright blue over the lake, and flies circle my head and even buzz the camera as I speak.

Let's just say that it's not a video that the "Pure Michigan" campaign will ever use.

I hiked up the incline to the lighthouse and dropped my pack at a picnic table. Dislodging what flies I could by swatting at myself and spinning in a circle (I call it my "crazy lady move"), I quickly ducked into the bathroom. At least thirty flies followed, but that was a great improvement. I took a few moments to swat at them, beating most of them dead, then I splashed cold water on my face and head to cool down.

I cleaned up as best I could, then toured the lighthouse and gift shop and chatted with the volunteer keepers. The lighthouse is unique in that it is square, not round. It gets its name from the location: 40 miles southeast of Old Mackinaw Point and 40 miles northwest of Thunder Bay. It was built in 1896.

About a hundred years later, the lighthouse was deteriorating and slated to be destroyed. The county stepped in and worked with the local lighthouse society to have the property conveyed to their jurisdiction. The unique structure still holds its place on the lakeshore only because of these groups working together to preserve this piece of history.

This story is repeated at almost any lighthouse you still see standing on the shores of the Great Lakes. Volunteers have raised money to restore the structures, then they run the gift shops and give tours during the warmer months. Some lighthouse societies raise enough money to employ permanent staff and sometimes even historians to curate the building and artifacts, to do research, and guide restoration.

I had already walked by Michigan's oldest lighthouse in Port Huron (the Fort Gratiot light built in 1829). It was undergoing restoration this year due to the efforts of the city and Friends of the Fort Gratiot Light group. The state of Michigan alone has 129 lighthouses remaining on its shores, and many vacationers go on lighthouse tours each year. I began this hike near the oldest light on the Great Lakes: Marblehead Lighthouse near Port Clinton, Ohio. It was built seven years before the Fort Gratiot light.

All together, the approximately 400 lighthouses that dot the Great Lakes stitch the shoreline with the history of the region and connect us to the past. In a time before GPS and radar and sonar, when people moved at the whim of the wind and then under the harnessed power of steam, these structures warned of shallows or rocky shoals, or guided vessels to take cover behind a sheltering point or to slip safely into a calm, deep harbor. I know of at least one light that is still maintained as a navigational aid by the Coast Guard. Most have been replaced, however, by steel towers mounted near the shoreline that have automated beacons. These are functional, but do not enhance our experience on the lakes or connect us to the past.

I left the 40-Mile Point Lighthouse and hiked on along the roads that led up to Rosalie's house. For whatever reason, the flies were not as bad along that stretch of road. Rosalie had an Australian shepherd named Zoe who checked me out carefully before allowing me into the house. After I had showered, put on clean clothes, and tossed all my sweaty, fly-smeared clothes into the washer, Rosalie shooed me upstairs to my room to take a rest.

I felt something hard underneath the pillow and pulled out a very large bone: Zoe's welcoming gift. The canine equivalent of a mint on the pillow.

After resting, Rosalie and I had a long chat about the things you're never supposed to talk about: politics and religion. Even though we didn't always agree on these topics, the discussion was lively and thoughtful. She has a keen mind, holds a Ph.D. in physics, but math was her first love.

The next morning, I walked with Rosalie, Zoe, and we stopped in at a neighbor's house to gather their two dogs to join us. Then Rosalie gave me a short ride north to a spot where I could hike the rest of the way to Cheboygan in one day.

## The vampire invader

In between Rogers City and Cheboygan is the Hammond Bay Biological Research Station. Here they work on how best to control the population of sea lamprey in the Great Lakes. This ancient fish could star in a horror movie. The lamprey can live in both fresh and sea water and grows to 20 inches in length. Okay, that might not be all that creepy, but consider its mouth: a round, suction cup opening lined with row after row of pointy teeth. They suction onto large fish, sink in their teeth, and literally suck the life out of them.

In 1955, the governments of the U.S. and Canada came together to form the Great Lakes Fishery Commission (GLFC). Its mandate was to find a way to control the lamprey, because they were chewing up the big fish in the Great Lakes, collapsing the fishery.

There was an article describing efforts to find a compound that would kill lamprey and not damage fish. This research was done in a very obvious way: place a rainbow trout, a bluegill and a larval lamprey in a jar of lake water and douse it with one of the trial chemicals. They did this for six years as they tested thousands of compounds. Reading the results of the test was simple: find the jar where the fish survived and the lamprey died. One compound worked, and Dow Chemical helped to refine the formulation and make it soluble in water. That chemical is 3-trifluromethyl-4-nitrophenol

(TFM for short).

I interviewed the supervisor of the research station, Dr. Mike Hansen, about the work being done there today.

"We still use TFM to treat lamprey spawning grounds," he told me. "This is our most effective tool in controlling the lamprey population. We briefly tried releasing sterilized males back into rivers to compete with native males at spawning, but the data showed that it wasn't an effective method. So we've moved on to other approaches."

"I've read about work to isolate pheromones to lure lamprey into traps. How is that going?"

"Well, there are various pheromones we are studying. The first is a migratory pheromone secreted by the larvae. It lets adults know that a stream has had successful spawning. Another is a mating pheromone secreted by males to attract the females."

He added that there is also a class of pheromones called necromones that repel lamprey. Current research is looking into ways to use necromones in certain streams to repel the lamprey, then to attract them to other streams with the attracting pheromones, where they would set up traps.

"How many lamprey are currently in the Great Lakes?" I asked.

"Adults? There are hundreds of thousands. If you're also counting larvae, there are millions."

"How many streams do you treat each year?"

"Of the 400 streams and rivers that are known lamprey breeding grounds, we treat about 200. We are continually monitoring lamprey populations and fish populations and collecting evidence of lamprey resurgence, so we can be responsive to what is going on in the lakes at any given time. We've also installed physical barriers in over 50 waterways to obstruct lamprey from moving into those tributaries and breeding."

"Sounds like a big job."

"It is. The Great Lakes Fishery Commission has a budget of $25 million a year to do research and control the lamprey. That may sound like a lot, but that investment protects the $7 billion fishing industry in the US and Canada."

I asked if this was being funded by fishing licenses, but he said, no, that all the funds come directly from U.S. and Canadian governments. The results are impressive: they've been able to reduce the lamprey population by 90% in most areas of the Great Lakes.

"Is there any hope of eradicating the lamprey completely?" I asked.

"Well, each female can lay up to 100,000 eggs, so it seems that consistent control is the key. It's a more realistic and attainable goal. Hopefully we'll continue to get better at it, like we've done ever since the GLFC was created."

If you are questioning the importance of the lamprey control team, think back to the 1960s when the Great Lakes fishery had crashed due to the predation of lamprey on large fish. With the biggest fish in the feeding chains nearly wiped out, smaller fish lower in the chain, like alewives, multiplied with fewer big fish around to feed on them. It is estimated that during the peak years of lamprey predation, 90% of the biomass in Lake Michigan was alewives, these little silver fish.

The major problem with alewives, from the point of view of anyone living or visiting the Great Lakes shorelines: during the spring, the alewives would often die off when the lake warmed. Their silver bodies were shoved in large numbers to the shoreline by waves, where they'd heap up in mounds to rot in the sun. Many communities had to use earthmoving equipment to gather up the millions of dead silvery fish and transported them to landfills or to farmlands where they could be used for fertilizer. But the wretched smell of rotting fish effectively crippled tourism along Great Lakes beaches for a decade. Through the control of the lamprey, along with the introduction of salmon, the Great Lakes fishery has been brought once again into tenuous balance.

I resumed my walk on US 23, which took me all the way to the city of Cheboygan, the last stop before I'd reach the top of Michigan's mitten. For the last ten miles or so, Bois Blanc Island was visible offshore, along with the Poe Reef light. "Bois Blanc" is French for "white wood." It may refer either to the white birch trees growing there or perhaps to the basswood trees found in the region.

On the side of the road, I found a huge, dead moth, a laurel sphinx. I picked it up to study it more closely. It was wider than my hand, measuring around 4 inches from one end of its wing tip to the other. The wings mimic the grain of wood, so it could blend in when clinging to a tree. As I held it in my hand, the long, white antennae were swept back from the head like rakish whiskers. It was beautiful. I took several photos, then set it carefully back into the roadside grasses.

## Bridge love

In northeast Michigan, there is a "rails-to-trails" project. The old Michigan Central Railroad bed has been converted to a trail topped with crushed gravel. I walked the portion that runs between the cities of Cheboygan and Mackinaw City. I took occasional detours out to the lakeshore to see if there was shoreline to walk, but rocky wetlands occupied every curve due to the sheltering effect of Bois Blanc Island and, as I got closer to the tip of Michigan, the narrowing of the waters that would form the Straits of Mackinac.

My first glimpse of the Mackinac Bridge made me feel like I was greeting an old friend. Bridges were magnificent markers along my journey: the Ambassador, the Blue Water, and now the Mighty Mac. Looking to the north, I could even make out the Grand Hotel on Mackinac Island situated east of the bridge. I decided to call my sister-in-law, Mary Jo. My niece, Alison, answered.

"Alison!" I said. "This is Aunt Loreen! Where's your mom?"

"Ah, hi," she said. "We're in the car. Mom's driving."

"I just wanted to tell her that I'm looking at Mackinac Island and the bridge!"

"Okay . . ." she said, sounding not enthused at all.

"You guys are coming up here in a couple weeks. We're going to the island! The bridge is one of the most beautiful bridges in the world!"

"Okay . . . I'll tell her." Clearly, she thought I was overreacting. Then I remembered that Alison had never been to this part of Michigan. She had never seen the bridge or been to Mackinac Island.

"I should go now," she mumbled.

"Sure. Bye." I figured she'd get excited once she got up there and saw the bridge spanning the peninsulas. She'd get a chance to ride her bike around the island and wade in the cold water of the straits.

Or maybe not. She and her brother, Julian, were teenagers after all. Maybe it wouldn't be cool to get excited by such amazing sites.

I walked on the straight, flat path for a couple more miles. These bike paths got me off the highway, but, yikes, could they be boring, as they followed the old railroad right-of-way, the flattest, straightest way between two points! At least highways went up and down hills, altering the view as I walked. I tried to pay more attention to the vegetation, studying the trees and plants along the way, and was delighted to find a large area overgrown with tall ferns. As I stopped to take a few photos, my phone rang. It was Mary Jo.

"You're at the bridge!" she yelled. "That's so cool! You're hiking so fast!"

Finally, the proper emotional response. "I know! I'm almost there. The bridge is gorgeous. And I can see the island, too."

"I love that bridge," she said. In the background, I could hear Alison and Julian mocking their mom's bridge love. She continued, in a voice that was a bit calmer. "These kids don't know how special that place is, but they will after this summer."

"I forgot they've never been up here," I said. They live in Georgia now, so when they come back to Michigan, their time is filled catching up with family instead of sightseeing.

"Are you going to the island now?" Mary Jo asked.

"No, I'll save that for when you guys are up here. Phil's coming up in a few days, and he'll take me home for a break before I meet up with you."

"I thought you were going to hike until we got there?"

I chuckled. "Well, it seems after about a month I need to go home and regroup." It was true. After a certain point, it helped enormously to be able to re-organize, refresh supplies, to put away the notes from one part of the hike, catch my breath, and push forward into the next.

"Understandably! Well, we're cleaning out the van for the big trip. We'll see you soon."

"Looking forward to it."

"Us, too. Bye!"


A few miles outside Mackinaw City, I came across the perfect branch on the side of the path to transform into a walking stick. I broke it off at the right length, stripped it of its bark with my knife, then took the rubber grip from my aluminum pole and whittled the top of the stick until I could snug the grip onto it. When I found a trashcan in Mackinaw City, I said farewell to my lightning rod and stuffed it into the trash.


## The wall: 300 miles

I had a few days before Phil would travel north to pick me up, so I took a day off in Mackinaw City. I was at 278 miles for the month and felt like I was pressing up against a wall, that breaking point for me where I would need to take a rest. My first month of hiking was just over 300 miles.

Was that my limit to do in one stretch?

And why did I feel that was a bad thing?

On my day off, I sought the answers to these questions by eating good food and fudge, and taking relaxing walks without my backpack strapped on my shoulders. I sat at a picnic table with a good view of the Mighty Mac Bridge, watching the freighters slip underneath the lofty metal span.

There is a disconnect that happens with a long hike. As a solo hiker, I experienced a separation from my normal world and was transported to where I existed to move along the lakeshore. I also felt a separation from any sense of home and from the people closest to me. The constant movement and the stripping down to the essentials also exposes the essential person you are. There is no need to clothe yourself to the occasion; you wear what you have with you. There is no easy retreat at the end of the day to your home; you are hundreds of miles from home with only what you can carry in your pack. There is no going backward; there is only the path that stretches ahead.

The result was a deep restlessness, a desire to keep moving. I found that even staying in one place for an extra day – a day off from the hike, something I typically looked forward to as I hiked – soon left me restless and longing to walk again. Even a stroll without my pack made me miss its weighty presence on my back.

The rest stops were only pauses on the walk. The hike, the constant movement alongside the water had become my home.

The next day I headed southwest, leaving the Straits of Mackinac and for the first time on this hike seeing the third Great Lake in my adventure: Lake Michigan. I headed toward Wilderness State Park. There, I found that all the cabins were rented for the night, so I pressed south toward tiny Cross Village. I was walking the road for a bit when an elderly gentleman stopped his truck and asked me how far I was going.

"Cross Village," I said.

"I'm headed that way," he said. "Climb in."

Since the day was hot and my pack heavy and I didn't feel like I needed to prove anything this day, I hopped into the truck. Frank told me he had grown up in the area, had hiked and hunted and fished in the region most of his 89 years.

"Have you seen many bear?"

"Never. They have this great nose," he said. "They'll know you're coming long before you get close." He thought for a moment, then turned and looked at me. "They lead a very special life."

He pointed out the places where the biggest deer lived and the lakes with the best fishing. When we passed by some dunes, he told me that he used to sled down them as a boy during the snowy winters. Frank's stories gave a sense of the importance of this wild place, the history attached to the little boy he once was, walking in the woods decades ago.

Frank stopped his truck in front of Legs Inn, the restaurant in Cross Village. I invited him to join me for dinner, but Frank had places to go. He took off with a wave.

Legs Inn is almost as old as Frank. In fact, he had told me that he remembered when they were building the place, and recalled when they had later added on certain parts of the stone structure. I had an excellent Polish dinner there – their specialty – sitting at an outside table overlooking Lake Michigan. Then I rented one of the tiny cabins down by the lakeshore.

That night was the first sunset I had seen on Lake Michigan during this hike. I felt like the world had re-aligned itself to the orientation most in tune with my inner compass.

## A snake, a crepe, and the perfect stream

I hiked the curving, rocky shoreline of Lake Michigan, headed south with the sun rising behind me. The land bulges here in a large arc into the lake. Farther south, it sucks itself back in between the towns of Harbor Springs and Petoskey to allow the lake to reach in and form Little Traverse Bay, separating these cities by water.

This arc of land is not much travelled. There are some summer homes sprinkled along here, so people come to the lake, but the shoreline is strewn with rocks in places and marshy in others, making a casual stroll morph into something more difficult.

It's a lovely stretch to walk, though, because of its variation and isolation. At times I moved through grasses and scrub bushes that come up to my waist. I tapped my walking stick on the ground to alert any snakes to my approach. I was tapping along when I noticed a snake about ten feet ahead of me. It was extended and had its head resting on the lower branch of a short plant. It looked awkward, like maybe a hawk dropped it there from a high height. I kept tapping my stick to see if it was alive, but it was motionless. I got closer and saw that it was a striped snake, brown, but the head isn't the triangle shape that would be characteristic of the only poisonous snake in Michigan: the Eastern Massasauga Rattler. I tapped right up to it and then, finally convinced it is dead, I touched it with my stick.

Fast-as-lightning, it curled into a defensive posture facing me.

That got my heart going!

It must have been snoozing in that stretched out position, relaxing and soaking up the morning sunshine until I happened along to poke it. I took some photos, still convinced that it was not a rattler. Its head was narrow and long. And even though it is coiled, it didn't do anything more than watch me.

I spoke calming words to it, apologized for the poke, then continued my walk.

I had never been to the small village of Good Hart that lies in between Cross Village and Harbor Springs, so I hiked up the hill to see what was there. Low and behold, there was a young guy in a tiny airstream trailer that is parked out in front of an antique store, and he was making crepes in there.

It is a little mobile creperie.

I order one with plump black cherries, sliced almonds, drizzled with chocolate, and topped with whipped cream. I sit outside to eat it with a cup of coffee and feel transported by the delicacy. I was still thinking about that snake I'd encountered on the way there. I found myself wishing I had brought the snake along with me and treated him to a crepe as an apology for waking him.

Later that hot day as I hiked along M-22, drawing closer to Harbor Springs, I realized that I was running low on water. I noticed a stream and hiked down the roadside toward it through thigh-high plants. I expected to kick up a lot of mosquitoes, but there were none; the stream is moving too quickly to harbor mosquito eggs. I get to the edge of the water and watch the stream curve through the land. It flows over a sand-and-stone bed, and over and under occasional logs in the waterway. The land is sloped, and the water crystal clear. It speaks as it hurries along, gurgling and murmuring, as it follows the decline of the land.

I kneel on the grassy bank and the scent of spearmint surrounds me. I study the nearby plants and, sure enough, spearmint grows wild here. I break off the top of one of the plants, pop the green leaves into my mouth and chew. Mint flavor fills my mouth, the freshest mint ever, often mimicked by chewing gum, but never fully captured like this.

Dumping bottle after bottle of stream water over my head refreshes me. The water is cold, the stream fed by springs, the flow from deep beneath the earth. I drink my fill, then soak my bandana and tie it, still dripping, around my neck. Then I recline on the banks of that stream on a bed of bent grasses scented with spearmint. I look up at the light blue sky and feel the stream water flowing inside me, even as I listen to it rush by.

Some of the best moments of my hike didn't involve moving at all.

Sometimes, the still, quiet bits were when everything snapped into focus.

These windows of being completely alive and present and content in the moment were gifts from this adventure.

# Early July

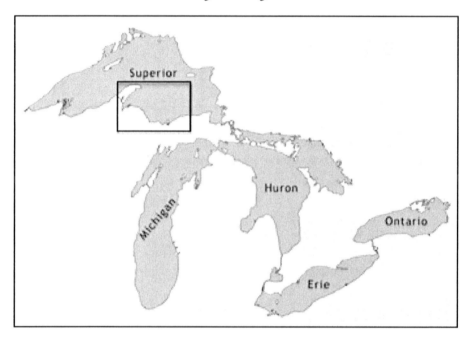

**Mackinac Island, Pictured Rocks National Lakeshore,
Estivant Pines Sanctuary, Copper Harbor;
Lake Huron and Lake Superior**

**77 miles in 6 days**

## Some time on Mackinac Island

In early July, I returned to Mackinaw City with my mom and my son, Ben. Mary Jo and her kids (Julian and Alison) and their good friend, Mary, joined us, and we boarded the ferry together.

Mary Jo manages a day care center for kids in Atlanta. She has the constant energy that a job like that requires. Her enthusiasm is contagious, though Julian and Alison, her teenage kids, steel themselves against it and try to maintain their casual slouch. Their friend and neighbor, Mary, is a proper Southern lady, long retired from working in the Governor's office in Atlanta. She has perfectly-done blondish hair and a warm, Southern drawl.

Since we caught an early morning ferry, our boat did a quick detour to pass underneath the Mackinac Bridge. I had crossed the bridge by car many times and had even walked the length of it one Labor Day, but this was the first time I had passed underneath it. The ferry was jammed with people, so our group had to split up to get seats. As we neared the bridge, cameras lifted and people snapped photos. Ben was sitting beside me, and we looked up at the looming structure as our boat slipped underneath it.

There is a certain amount of bravado that a bridge builder must possess to think they can loft steel over a gap of open water. Bridges don't easily leap, especially over a gap as wide and wild as the Straits of Mackinac. For many years, a bridge here was considered impossible: the water is too deep, the lakebed too unstable, the currents in the straits too strong, the wind too unpredictable. All of this is true, but somehow it was overcome by the elegant design of a bridge that could finally stitch together the two peninsulas of Michigan.

Our ferry circled the base of one of the towers and the bridge momentarily floated over the boat, then we turned toward Mackinac Island. At this point you may be questioning my ability to spell the name of the bridge, the island, the straits, and the city.

*Why does she keep going back and forth between spellings? Who is her editor?*

Calm down. That's just the way it is.

The French used the Native American word for the island, and the French spelled Mackinac with the terminal "c" which the French pronounced as a *"w."* Both spellings, in fact, are pronounced the same, as *Mack-in-aw,* regardless of how it is spelled. When the British and Americans took over the area, they used the same name, but changed the spelling. The island, straits, and bridge use the French spelling (Mackinac), the city (Mackinaw City) the British. I agree, it's a little confusing, but there you have it.

Our ferry unloaded its cargo of people and luggage at the dock on Main Street. We walked through the crowds to Marquette Park and then went to the art museum. The museum has exhibits that relate to the island, and my favorite part is a room filled with early maps of the Great Lakes region where the mitten of Michigan looks all smushed and pulled to the side. The earliest maps here were made by French voyageurs who travelled these waters in canoes. That the maps resemble modern maps at all is the amazing thing when you consider the limited measurement tools they had to use. How they were able to interpret distance and shoreline from a canoe (factoring in current and wind) and then come up with a reasonable picture of the lakes is amazing. Lake Superior is especially accurate on some of the maps, even when Michigan's mitten is distorted.

We rode bikes around the island, enjoying the summer day, the bright clear sunshine, and the company of family. My mom and Mary went off to check out the shops. Before leaving the island, we took another ride around it on bikes, but after the island had emptied of the day-trippers. Alison thought it was a race, so she took off on her bike and we didn't see her until we returned to the town at the end, but Mary Jo, Ben and I caught up to Julian and rode near him most of the way.

At one point during our evening ride, I pulled up alongside Julian to chat as we rode. "I'm coming up to talk to you, don't be alarmed," I said as I matched his speed. This got a small smirk from him. Julian is rather shy, and I gently tease him about that to ease the tension. Then I asked, "So what do you think of the island?"

"I like it," he said. "Cooler than stuff in Georgia."

"Well, Georgia doesn't have all this water. I missed that when we lived in Atlanta."

He nodded.

"Have you looked at the rocks here?" I said pointing up to the craggy gray rocks protruding from the hillside. He shook his head.

"It's limestone. Very old limestone. And it's filled with fossils because it was formed by ancient coral reefs when the entire state was covered in a shallow sea."

He looked a little interested, but not enough to get more than another nod. I knew I had to get on another topic to get him to talk, so I brought up soccer, a sport that both he and Alison excelled at. That got him to say a few sentences. After a little conversation we were soon back in town and ready for dinner.

## The British Landing

The War of 1812 encroached on this island. There had been a fort on the island for many years prior to the war. First it was the rustic Fort Holmes, then the larger Fort Michilimackinac was built, the fortification that still stands on the island today, its white walls topping the hill above Marquette Park. The island is a strategic place to hold, as it overlooks the Straights of Mackinac where Lake Michigan flows into Lake Huron.

When war was declared in June of 1812, the Americans on the island didn't hear about it before British and Native Americans invaded the island one month later. The British placed two cannons on the high ground in the middle of the island, and surrounded the fort with troops and warriors. The American garrison feared that the villagers would be slaughtered if they put up a fight, so they surrendered the fort. The place where the invaders came ashore is called British Landing; a historical marker denotes the site today along the path around the island.

Two years later the Americans tried to take back the fort using the same tactics, but they were unsuccessful.

In 1814, the war was at its darkest point for the Americans. The British had invaded Washington City (as it was called at the time) and burned many of the buildings there, including the White House, Capitol Building (still under construction at the time), the Library of Congress, and the Treasury Building. The most famous story coming out of this tragedy is that of Dolly Madison, the First Lady, refusing to leave the White House without the portrait of George Washington. She saved that symbol of the new nation from the flames at a time when the survival of the new nation was in peril.

## The most superior lake

My son Ben and I left the island after having breakfast with the group. Mary Jo, my mom and Mary were heading off to the Grand Hotel to have a look around, and Julian and Alison were going to do some shopping before they had to leave the island. We hugged everyone, then headed to the docks to catch our ferry.

Ben's long, auburn hair whipped around in the wind on the top deck of the ferry, and I snapped several photos with his hair dancing behind him. After graduating from high school (where there was a mandate that boy's hair stay short), Ben had let his hair grow, so that it now reached the middle of his back.

We drove over the Mackinac Bridge and headed north through the Upper Peninsula. Our destination was the small town of Grand Marais on the shores of Lake Superior, the fourth Great Lake I would hike along on this adventure. Pictured Rocks National Lakeshore begins to the west of Grand Marais and spans the distance between it and the next town on the lake, a place called Munising.

We planned to hike the entire length (over 40 miles) in four days. The rule in a national lakeshore area (as in national parks and any state park) is to not remove anything – even a small rock – so Ben and I got our rock hound fix at Agate Beach in Grand Marais before beginning our hike.

## Magic rocks

Agates are magical rocks. Okay, this is not the technical, geological definition, but I think it captures the nature of these rocks better than saying they are a variegated form of chalcedony. Chalcedony (pronounced *kal-SED-nee*) is a type of quartz, a microcrystalline quartz, made of silicon dioxide. But it's easier to say that they are among the most magical of rocks.

Now, I have a background in the sciences, and I even took a geology course to better understand the Great Lakes region, but sometimes the experience of finding a rock like an agate, plucking it out of the water and holding it close so you can see the delicate banding and layer upon layer of colors, is more satisfying in the moment – *This is the most beautiful rock!* – than all the scientific theories about how they were formed.

Being a scientist, though, I did want to know how this rock came to be, how the beach here became filled with such a wide variety of colorful stones, and, yes, how the magical agate was formed.

The geology of Lake Superior is considerably different from the other lakes. It is the oldest of the Great Lakes, predating the ice sheets that formed the lower lakes. And there is a rift zone, called the Keweenawan rift, running along the northern edge of Michigan's Upper Peninsula. This rift was volcanically active about one billion years ago. All that lava welling up from the earth's mantle marked the area. There are entire books written about the geology of the Keweenaw Peninsula, and the oldest fossils ever found on earth, stromatolites, have been found here.

But back to the agates. There are several theories about the formation of agates, but most agree that there has to be a void or hole in the rock that is slowly filled with layer after layer of silica (carried in minute amounts by water passing through the rocks) filling in the void. Then, under the proper conditions of pressure and time and temperature, an agate may form. The color in each band can be due to impurities (iron and aluminum are most common) or in the way the fibers of the minerals are twisted within each band.

Another theory is that molten silica blobs formed in the lava, then were compressed over millions of years to squeeze them into agates.

Ben and I waded in the cool water on Agate Beach in Grand Marais, scooping up handfuls of rocks and plucking various specimens out to slip into our pockets. We saw cloudy quartz, rhyolite, jasper, granite, chert, shale, and fossilized coral in almost every handful. The colors dazzled: red, burgundy, green, translucent white, black, orange, gray and brown.

I found one agate, a small one about the size and shape of an almond. The colors of the bands were muted, off-white and gray and brown, subtly shifting in intensity from band to band.

I showed it to Ben.

"Yay! You got one," he said.

"Keep it." I handed it to him, and he studied it closely.

"Nope. I've got to find my own." With that, he handed it back to me and scooped up another handful of rocks.

An agate is translucent; it allows light to pass through it. This is one of the ways to pick out agates from other rocks. On sunny days, they appear to "glow" as the sunlight works its way into them. An agate sliced thin allows light to stream through, illuminating its colored bands. If you walk around the town of Grand Marais, you'll see agates used as decorations everywhere. Even the B&B where we stayed the night before our hike began, The Agate Cross, had a bunch of them glittering in the windows.

The sliced rock resembles a gorgeous piece of stained glass, but it is ancient, organized, crystallized minerals. And the fact that it was formed underground over millions of years, well, that seems a little magical, doesn't it?

Lake Superior got its name because it is geographically "superior" or "above" the other lakes, but it is certainly superior in many other ways. It is the largest, the coolest, the deepest of the Great Lakes. It is so large, in fact, that it contains more water than the other four Great Lakes combined. It is also the cleanest of the lakes by virtue of its size, its remoteness (there are fewer people and less industrialization on its shores), and the fact that it is upstream from the other lakes.

I had decided that I wanted to hike the length of Pictured Rocks National Lakeshore as part of my Lake Superior leg of this adventure. It is not only a beautiful, dramatic area of the lake, but it is historically important, as this was the very first stretch of shoreline in America to get this national designation and protection back in 1966.

## Ben at my side

We parked the car at the National Lakeshore's visitor center at the east end of the park and grabbed our stuffed backpacks out of the trunk. We'd leave the car here, take a shuttle to the other end of the park, and hike back to the car. My pack now had things strapped to the outside since we were using a two-person tent (which was bulkier than my hammock tent) and sleeping pads. I was also carrying all the food we'd need for our four-day hike. And I had slipped a paperback of short stories by William Faulkner into my pack. We wrestled our packs onto the shuttle and took seats near the back. The shuttle dropped us near the city of Munising for the start of our hike. In about an hour, we rode the miles we would walk over the next four days.

Shouldering our backpacks, we hiked east through the forest for the first part of the day, then the trail came to the lake and began hugging the top of sandstone cliffs. We could see Grand Island in the bay for most of the day. Amazingly, there wasn't a breeze coming off the lake. I thought this was an impossibility – surely the warm air sitting over the cool water would set up some sort of convection currents and move the air around a bit! Not this day.

There are lakeshore boat tours that leave from Munising, and we saw these white, double decker boats motoring back and forth, parallel to the 200-foot tall escarpment. When the boats passed nearby, we were better able to grasp the scale of the cliffs we were on and the distance to Grand Island. Along the trail, there were many vantage points where we could see intricately sculpted sandstone formations: Miners Castle and Chapel Rock are two of the most famous.

The area is called "Pictured Rocks" because mineral-rich water leaches out of the sandstone, creating colorful streaks on the rock face. Black is manganese, the red and orange is iron, the yellow and brown is limonite, and copper streaks the sandstone face green. Over thousands of years, "paintings" have developed, intense and vibrant in some areas, and subtle and ethereal in others. In places where the sandstone has fractured and fallen away, the newly exposed rock is lighter in color, unblemished, a fresh canvas for the migrating minerals.

The force of the water moving through the sandstone, freezing and thawing each time the temperature dips, creates fractures in the bluffs. There are many places where the top of the bluff overhangs a void where the rock below has flaked away. There were warnings along the trail not to venture too close to the edge, as there was danger that weak spots could fall away under the added weight of a hiker. In fact, one of the rangers told us that a short section of the trail had fallen into the lake just the week before we arrived.

Thankfully, no one was on top when it plunged 200 feet into the cold depths of Lake Superior.

I'm sure many people look at the sandstone bluff and think that it's been unchanged for tens of thousands of years, but this area is quite young, geologically speaking. The entire Great Lakes basin has only looked the way it looks today for a few thousand years. That's a blink in geological time. And the sandstone cliffs in Pictured Rocks are constantly wearing away, flaking and fracturing, subtly transforming. One of the most famous formations, Miner's Castle, has changed so radically that it is possible to see the transformation documented in drawings and even in recent photos. In a drawing for an article published in Harper's Magazine in 1867, the "castle" has two very large "turrets" on the top. A photo from 1971 shows the same turrets, but worn down considerably. In April 2006, one of the turrets collapsed into the lake. Fishermen in the area at the time called park rangers on their cell phones to let them know about the avalanche of rock.

When water freezes, the molecules become organized, and the ice will swell to 10% larger than the original mass of the liquid water. That may not seem like much, but I'm sure you've frozen a sealed container of water or can of pop at some point and experienced the force of this expansion. Imagine water filling a crack in the rock, freezing and thawing many times, widening that gap each time. It is a persistent and relentless attack on the integrity of these bluffs. This force has contributed to the sculpting of the formations, along with wind and wave action. Even tree roots work their way into the gaps in the stone and contribute to the process.

It was 80 degrees or hotter each day we hiked these pictured rocks. We crossed over many streams and took time to keep our water bottles filled and our bandanas soaked. Some streambeds were dry, as the water table had lowered in the warm summer with little precipitation.

Most of the first day's hike was in the woods and on top of the bluff overlooking the cool, vast lake. It was tantalizing to see that water – clear and in colors ranging from turquoise and greens near the shore, dark blue and black farther out where it dropped off to depths of hundreds of feet – but not be able to soak our feet or swim in it to cool off. A mile or so before we reached our first campsite, though, we descended to Miners Beach, a wide, sandy expanse on the lakeshore.

We shrugged off our heavy packs, slipped into our swimsuits, then plunged into the cool water. Even after submerging several times, I could place my hand on the top of my head and feel the heat radiating off my head through my wet hair.

After our swim, we hiked the length of the beach barefoot, enjoying the feel of soft sand on our wet feet. Then, we laced up our boots to hike up the bluff to our first campsite in the Potato Patch area. The trail hugs interior dolomitic sandstone walls that are white and pockmarked with shallow caves. The campground is on top of this ridge, and I felt each step up the steep trail tug at the core of my body. We reached the camping area and chose a site near the edge of the bluff, overlooking the lake through a partial screen of skinny trees.

A ranger appeared out of nowhere just as we had finished putting up our tent. He was in full uniform, and strapped on his utility belt were a Taser gun and a real gun in addition to many other outdoorsy gadgets.

"Can I see your permit," he said, not asking. It was attached to the bottom of my backpack.

"Here it is." I held it out to him.

He looked at it, verified that we were supposed to be there that night and had paid the proper fees, then he flipped it over and pointed to one of the rules on the back. "You're supposed to pitch your tent within 15 feet of this post." He pointed to the post. "Your tent is too far away."

"Sorry," I said, estimating in my head that it was probably 17 feet away. "We just chose the flattest part of the site with the fewest roots. We'll move it closer."

He still looked pretty concerned about the infraction, even though I had already begun to pull up the tent stakes.

"Anyone else in the campground tonight?" I asked, hoping to direct his rule-following compulsion elsewhere.

"One other site should be occupied tonight." He looked around a bit, as sweat trickled from underneath his hat and down the side of his face. "Good night, then." With that he walked off to find the other campers.

"Yikes," I say to Ben when he had gone. "I thought he might taze me for the infraction."

"Oh, mom," Ben sighed. Ben is a rule follower and probably would have sided with the ranger.

"We need more water to cook with." I pulled out a plastic bag and grabbed my nearly empty water bottle.

"I'll hike back down to the lake," Ben said.

"I'll come."

"I've got it, mom." He smiles at me.

I am relieved that I don't have to hike back down and up from the beach again. I am, quite frankly, whipped from the day . . . mostly the heat, but also from hiking with the extra-heavy pack for ten miles. Since there were two of us, I had left my hammock tent at home, opting for the heavier two-person tent for this part of the hike. And sleeping in a tent meant we'd be sleeping on the ground, so we each packed a thick pad to put underneath our sleeping bags.

"Thanks," I said to Ben. "I'll get dinner set up and finish moving the tent."

It is strange to split up the camping chores. I had been on my own for so long.

After dinner and getting ready to sleep, I stored our food and toothpaste and things in the nearby bear box.

With a name like "bear box," I always expect to find a bear *inside* the box when I open it.

We watch the sun descend into the lake for a bit, and a rabbit hops around our campsite. She is curious and not too afraid during her visit. The sunlight lights up her ears so they glow atop her head, the fine blood vessels streaking red lines within the thin membrane of her delicate, translucent ears.

After the sun had submerged in the lake, we limp into our tent and settle in for the night. In a few minutes I heard Ben's breathing slow as he gives in to deep sleep.

I stay awake for a long time listening to the night sounds. It is strange sleeping on the ground; I am usually suspended above it in my hammock tent. Every time I begin to drift off to sleep, a chipmunk races toward the tent through dry leaves and the primitive part of my brain screams *STAMPEDE!* and I jerk awake, heart thudding.

I finally curse the chipmunks and the thrashing deer and stuff bits of tissue in my ears as crude earplugs so I can sleep.

## A chapel made of rock

The elevation changes on the trail the next day were more extreme. We gained some gorgeous views up the lakeshore, along with a unique perspective on the Pictured Rocks we had only seen previously from lake level. Chapel Rock is beautiful and curious, a beautifully sculpted pedestal with several ornate columns supporting the top slab. It is a remnant of Cambrian Age sandstone, shaped mostly by water when the lake level was much higher. On top of the rock, an ancient white pine tree grows. This tree has been there for around two centuries. It was mentioned in the journals of early explorers, including Douglass Houghton on his travels looking for clues pointing to the rich copper and iron deposits in the Upper Peninsula.

The most curious feature of Chapel Rock is that the roots of the tree span a gap between the free-standing formation and the nearby cliff. The thick roots twine around each other as they stretch through the air. The reason for this oddity: at one time, there was an archway connecting the formation to the nearby cliff. But it broke away fifty years ago, leaving the roots unsupported in their reach for sustenance. The pine tree still thrives atop the formation. Despite the harsh, Lake Superior winters, it has grown to almost equal the height of its ornate pedestal.

We had a better appreciation for the scale of these cliffs from the top, looking down their striated and streaked faces. A few times the trail led down to near the water level, to a sandstone shelf that reached out into the lake. We took these opportunities to gather water and study the layers of sandstone sculpted by water, wind, and time.

Wild flowers bloomed in the shady woods, and we even saw a strange, ghostly, parasitic plant called Indian Pipe (*Monotropa uniflora)*. This plant is waxy and white and has droopy flowers. It is strangely eerie-looking because it has no chlorophyll. It survives by extracting nutrients from fungi growing on tree roots. We came across a little line of these "pipes" poking out of the woodland debris. They were a few inches tall and were unlike any plant we had ever seen.

If you've taken the boat tour of Pictured Rocks, you might assume that the sandstone cliffs continue on and on, long past the part you toured. Not so. After rounding Grand Portal Point, the cliffs gradually become more diminutive, then subsume into an area with several pretty coves, then they disappear entirely into a long stretch called Twelve Mile Beach, a lovely sandy beach that stretches for a dozen miles along Lake Superior.

Ben and I waded in the coves area, where sandstone escarpments lifted barely twenty feet above the lake and sandstone flats reached far out underneath the water. These submerged slabs were beautiful with ridges and holes sculpted by waves. Multi-colored pebbles filled the depressions and gathered in any ridge or fissure they found. We studied these beautiful sights through the clear lake water. The water gently rippled and then bounced off the sandstone cliff, making complex wave interactions. These undulations refracted and bent the sun's rays as they passed through the water, illuminating the underwater rock with constantly changing patterns of light.

Tired, sore and parched, I bent down and stuck my face into the clear, cool waters of Lake Superior and drank until I was no longer thirsty.

"Did you drink?" Ben asked, alarmed.

"I couldn't take it anymore. All this clean water, and all day we've been squeezing and sucking on a filtering bottle. I snapped."

Ben shook his head and continued following the rules to avoid drinking from streams or from the lake.

We set up camp, careful to pitch our tent near the designated post. We ate dinner, stored our food in the bear box, and went to sleep as the sun set.

While we didn't see any bear on our hike, I remembered a story from a friend, Bill, who had hiked this same path many years ago.

"I was hiking it with my buddy. He's a real skinny guy," Bill said. "To tell you how much I knew about backpacking, I took along a canned ham!

"A small one, but still. Not the wisest choice." He shook his head, remembering the weight of that ham in his pack. "One night we were setting up and cooking dinner. I had set my tent on the other side of the fire from my buddy's tent, and I was leaning over the fire cooking when my buddy whispered, 'Bill, look over there.' Well, I turned and saw this huge black bear right by my tent."

"What did you do?"

"I took up the lids from the pots and started banging them together to make a big racket."

"Did that work?" I asked.

"Nope. That bear stood up on its hind legs and stared down at me. I was the chubby guy in the group, you see."

I laughed.

"Well, my skinny buddy had this loud shout he could do. So he let loose with one, and that bear turned on its heels and ran out of camp."

"What happened then?"

"I moved my tent right next to my buddy's," Bill laughed. "The next day we were hiking. It was early spring, and we met this Native American on the trail. He had to be seven feet tall and had a chainsaw and a can of gas slung over his shoulders. Working on trail maintenance.

"We told him about the huge bear and how we had such a fright.

"This tree of a man looked down at us and laughed, 'That was just old Sally! You probably scared the daylights out of that old sow!'"

Old Sally was probably no longer around. Nor were her descendants, as far as we could tell. But we still used the bear boxes faithfully, not wanting to experience a close encounter with a big black bear, no matter how shy or well-known to the locals she might be.


## A lion beetle

The third day hiking with Ben featured very few rocks, pictured or plain. We hiked most of the day along the beautiful 12-mile beach that forms the middle part of the National Lakeshore. It was nice to get away from the forest and to walk right at the edge of this greatest of Great Lakes.

The lake was still unnaturally calm this day, with only ripples disturbing its surface. There were still many stretches where sandstone shelves peeked out of the sand or ran alongside the beach, submerged, for a long ways out into the lake. We saw a great blue heron and a bald eagle flying along the water's edge. A bit later, we spotted a group of merganser ducks hanging out on shore, before taking off onto the lake when they noticed us. We waded through a couple rocky streams merging with the lake. Near one, Ben noticed a huge water beetle, about two inches long and one inch wide. It was a lot of beetle!

"Let's take a picture," I said. "Do you want to hold the beetle, or take the camera?"

Ben stared down at the huge beetle. "Ahhhh, camera."

I picked up the beetle and Ben took several photos of its black underbelly, striped with orange markings that resembled huge eyes. He got a close-up of its strange front legs with its flattened and cupped joints that enable it to skate on the surface of the water. Turns out it was a predacious water beetle, the lion of the pond, hanging out on the surface before diving down to attack its prey.

We sat on a sandstone outcropping for a break and watched dark clouds build in the distance. Miles away, rain was falling, but still no waves were forming on the unusually calm lake. We hustled to our campground, Benchmark, and manage to set up camp, take a swim, and eat while the rain clouds gathered in the late afternoon.

When the rain began to fall, we covered our packs with trash bags and got comfortable inside the tent. Since there was plenty of light, we took turns reading my favorite short story by William Faulkner, "Spotted Horses," to each other from the thin paperback I had brought along. It is a long, short story, so I read a few pages, then handed the book off to listen a bit while Ben read to me. This is one of my favorite short stories, and it was wonderful to hear it in Ben's deep voice. I was transported back to those times reading to my boys when they were young.

Once the rain had passed, we emerged to make a snack before bedtime.

During the night, the rainfly on the tent began to glow with a penetrating soft light. Since it had stormed that day and was still quite warm, I assumed it was heat lightning somewhere out on the lake. Without putting on my glasses, I watched the blur of light moving around the rain fly. It was soothing, and even seemed to change colors over time. I fell back to sleep, watching it and listening to the lake murmuring on the other side of a low dune. Days later, I would realize that these were the Northern Lights, when someone I encountered back in town mentioned how bright they had been on this particular night.

Most of our gear was dry by the time we packed up the next day and headed toward the lighthouse. Every lighthouse in the Great Lakes marks a place of danger to ships, and often also marks a safe harbor. In the early 1800s – before there were many lights to guide the sailing ships – shipwrecks were common. Part of the decision process for where to construct lighthouses was based on where ships were wrecking with some frequency, so many of the lights also mark the graves of boats and their crew. Even after lights were erected on these dangerous shores, some ships were still lost, tragically, near these welcoming beacons, during thick fog or heavy seas.

As Ben and I hiked through such a fog to the Au Sable Light Station, located on a small point not far from the east end of Twelve Mile Beach, we encountered a sign listing ten notable wrecks that had taken place at Au Sable Point. Some boats had been saved and refloated after running aground, while others were a total loss. We walked a short path from the trail to the lakeshore, where we could look into the clear water to see the timbers of ships more than a century old still resting there. The long hull of a steam barge, the *Mary Jarecki,* rested perpendicular to the shore, barely submerged. It was a steam barge that went down on July 4, 1883. Its presence disrupted the currents in the lake, and now the waves zigzagged into each other over the top of it, outlining its final resting place. A few iron spikes protruded above the water, periscopes from the past.

Another wreck was submerged farther out. The movement of the water did not give away its presence, but if we looked closely, we could see the ghostly forms of its strong timbers. The massive beams seemed to undulate and quiver, but it was only the distortion of the moving water that would forever engulf it.


## Recognition

We went into the lighthouse gift shop to talk to the ranger and volunteer worker. I wanted to ask which route we should take to get past the massive dune that flanked the shoreline east of the lighthouse.

I started with Phyllis, the volunteer, a fit woman in her 60s.

"We're hiking to the Grand Marais Visitor Center today and wondered if it's possible to hike at the water's edge all the way past the dune."

"Let's ask the ranger." Phyllis called her over.

The ranger didn't know for certain, but knew that it was how the keepers used to hike to town, at the foot of the dune. "I don't know if it's passible now," she said, "and the fog's too thick to see much of anything today."

"I'd really like to hike at the water's edge if possible," I said.

"But if you reach a point where the dune ends in deep water, you'll have to turn around and climb back up the log slide," the ranger said. Between us and the town of Grand Marais was a spot called the log slide, because there was once a wooden chute that guided logs on their way down to the lake.

Ben sucked in a breath at the thought of climbing up hundreds of feet of a sand dune. "We don't want to do that."

The ranger wished us good luck as she prepared to open the buildings for visitors. I was fixated on finding out if the hike along the water was possible.

"Is there anyone who would know? Anyone you could call?" I asked Phyllis.

"Not that I can think of," Phyllis said. "Why is it so important to walk by the water?"

"I'm doing a 1,000-mile hike touching all of the Great Lakes. And I like to stay close to the—"

"Did you hike around Lake Michigan?"

"Yes."

"Hey! I heard you speak in Madison, Wisconsin!"

"And you didn't recognize me?" I gestured at myself, knowing how grubby I looked after three days on the trail.

"Well," Phyllis chuckled, "you didn't recognize me, either!"

We all laughed. We visited a little longer, then Ben and I pulled out our journals and Phyllis opened up the stamp pad with red ink. They had several stamps available that people could use to commemorate their visit by stamping their National Parks Passport. Ben and I chose to have our journals stamped with the fine image of the Au Sable Light Station flanked by trees, all in red ink.

"At the top of the log slide, you'll be able to see way up the shoreline if the fog lifts," Phyllis said.

Ben and I wandered in between the buildings at the light station and snapped a few photos of the lighthouse before pressing on into the woods.

The hike from the lighthouse to the top of the log slide had the most abrupt elevation change we had encountered. The lighthouse is at lake level, while the log-slide dune towers 300 feet above the lake. The two places are only about a mile and a half apart, and most of the climbing takes place in the last half mile. For that last bit, it's like climbing the stairs to the top of a 30-story building. My legs were burning when we were halfway up, and I suggested we take a break. Ben gamely stopped, though I don't think he much needed it. When we finally got to the top, we shrugged off our heavy packs and leaned them against a signpost while we checked out the dune.

It is strange to stand on a 300-foot dune overlooking the largest freshwater lake (by surface area) in the world. This specific dune is a perched dune, formed atop a glacial moraine. That means it is not pure sand all the way through, but sand on top, with clay and rocks underneath the covering of sand that has blown up onto it. This also allows it to be steeper than a dune made of pure sand. Standing on it, I felt like I would tumble down to the lake if enough of the sand gave way beneath my feet.

This area is called the log slide because there was once a wooden chute that guided logs on their way down to the lake. It is said that the sliding logs would create enough friction that the chute would occasionally burst into flames. Ben hiked along the face of the dune a bit. I looked out into the foggy lake for a moment, then looked back toward Ben. I had lost him. He was swallowed up by the scale of the dune, and his auburn hair and tan clothes blended perfectly with the color of the sand. It was only when he turned his head that I was able to locate him again.

Ben and I walked toward each other and stopped. The fog clung to the shoreline we wanted to hike, and a low cloud obscured even the top of this dune that curved for miles toward the city of Grand Marais.

"What do you think?" I asked.

"I don't think we should risk it." Ben gestured to the steep path at our feet leading down to the lake. "If it's impassable, we'll have to hike back up right here."

He was correct. The shoreline between the lighthouse and us was rocky and fell into deeper water at times, and there wasn't any place on this massive dune that was better to climb than the log slide. I wanted to hike the shoreline, but knew I'd have a hard time making it back up the dune with my pack, and suspected Ben didn't want to do that either. I squinted, trying to penetrate the fog. I willed it to clear, but it didn't work. I thought of offering to split up: I take the lake route, Ben takes the woods, but I didn't want to separate, not after matching our strides for the past three days. We had found a good rhythm together, and I wanted to share every moment I could with him. Ben was going to move to Pittsburgh in the fall to begin graduate school; he was setting off on his adult life.

"We'll take the trail," I said.

"Okay," Ben said with a sigh of relief.

We hiked the trail the rest of the day. We passed through mature forests and fields of ferns tucked behind the massive shoreline dune. The wall of sand insulated us from any lake sounds, and at one point we were hiking through a large forest nestled in a gentle bowl of the land. I noticed the quiet and suggested we sit for a bit. I found a felled tree that was at a good sitting height and shrugged off my pack. I grabbed my water bottle and sat down and Ben joined me.

The absence of sound was remarkable. There was a loamy layer of decayed leaves underfoot that quieted the movements of even the stampeding chipmunks. A few small birds flitted through the trees, but silently, never even chirping to each other. We calmed our breathing and listened to the silence while we shared the water.

On the hike, we had encountered many fallen or decaying beech trees. Most of them were overgrown with destructive fungus, something caused by an invasive bark scale brought over from Europe. The scale doesn't kill a tree on its own, but makes it susceptible to overwhelming infection by the fungi. We saw many beech trees in our silent forest glen that were covered with various forms of fungi, sometimes dotting the trunk of the tree from ground level to heights of over fifteen feet. There were warnings posted at several places in the park about not setting up camp too near these dying trees because they might topple over in the slightest wind.

Our hike skirted Grand Sable Lake (a kettle lake, formed in a depression created by the retreating glaciers), then passed through fields abloom with wild flowers. Finally, we reach the Grand Marais visitor center where we had left my car four days earlier. I was a bit punchy from the hike and the heat and the 35 pounds on my back by the time we saw the car. We giddily shot some photos. Then I linked arms with Ben and began singing the "We're off to see the Wizard" song from that movie, doing the skip-hop-step dance with my son and our backpacks up the path. Ben didn't know the steps, but he gamely let me drag him along as I sang.

We drove to the town of Grand Marais and had dinner at the West Bay Diner. I had a BLT club sandwich that was the best BLT I have ever had. Ben had some gigantic sandwich and a chocolate shake. We kept smiling at our sandwiches, still a bit giddy, and then at each other, happy to have survived our time in the wild.

## The Keweenaw

After our dinner, we drove west, heading for Copper Harbor, a town located at the tip of the Keweenaw Peninsula poking out into Lake Superior. There are only a few places in Michigan where you can walk through forests that were spared from Michigan's lumbering decades. One of these is up on the peninsula near Copper Harbor, a place called the Estivant Pine Sanctuary. I wanted to walk among the giants there. Another reason to hike the Keweenaw is the astonishing geology you'll find there. You may think I'm overreacting, but it's true: the geology of this stubborn peninsula that juts so boldly and so far out into Lake Superior is truly astonishing.

First of all, a billion years ago there was a mid-continental rift that sliced through where Lake Superior now exists. That rift was pulling apart and oozing lava, spewing lava on and off for a couple of million years, pouring out molten basalt from miles beneath the surface, forming an ever-widening rift valley. After all that lava cooled, the earth's crust sagged underneath the weight of it, shaping Lake Superior's basin.

This was eons before glaciers ever plowed through the region, which was a more recent force that left its mark across the region. And think about it: the Keweenaw juts out for miles into Lake Superior, having withstood the onslaught of those mile-high sheets of ice.

If you ever have occasion to fly over Lake Superior, notice how both the Keweenaw and Isle Royale have striations – ridges – running in the same direction. This is because they are the two edges of this basin, a *syncline* formation that rises above the water. You are basically looking at a cross-section of the earth's crust here. It has been broken and tilted upward so that layer upon layer of the crust is exposed as ridges in the land. This formation is why Lake Superior is so much deeper than the other Great Lakes.

In fact, Lake Superior holds more water than the other four lakes combined. Its deepest point is over 1,300 feet deep.

The Keweenaw is known for something else: copper. During long periods where the flow of lava was molten gave time for the melted copper to pool together in pure form. Copper is veined throughout the land here and even under the water. There are sites where large boulders of copper were found sitting on riverbanks. This copper was long prized by the Native Americans and prehistoric people before them. They mined it to use for tools and ornaments and for trade throughout North America. The copper they found was often so pure they could just hammer it out and shape it for use without having to refine it. It is estimated that Native Americans pulled up to 500 million pounds of copper out of the Keweenaw and Isle Royale mines over a thousand years.

If that seems like an enormous amount (and it is), consider that since Michigan became a state in 1837, mining companies have extracted over twenty times that quantity of that elemental metal, still as valued by us today as it was for the Native Americans.

So Ben and I headed to the tip of the Keweenaw. We wanted to see the basalt hills that tell of a time when the earth split open, spewed magma, and then collapsed to form the bottom of a Great Lake.

We checked into a B&B with a view of Lake Superior and I called first shower.

A shower! After four days of hiking!

Ben's phone had a signal, so he called his girlfriend. After a long and refreshing rinse, I flopped into my fluffy bed, wondering why anyone would ever choose to sleep on the ground with stampeding chipmunks and dreams of bears named Sally. It seemed a bit crazy until I remembered the beauty and isolation of the Pictured Rocks, the sandstone cliffs both rising above and plunging into the pure waters of the most superior of lakes.

I arranged my four pillows in the perfect way to sleep surrounded by comfort, then fell asleep to dream about the wonders of Lake Superior.

## A sanctuary of pines

We only had one day to hike the Keweenaw, so we headed out after breakfast to the pines sanctuary. On the dirt road we took there, the woods were being logged. If you've never seen a modern logging operation, let me tell you that it is far removed from the forest sawyers and river rats of the past. You hardly see the people anymore because they are tucked into the control cabs of massive machinery that powerfully cuts the trees, strips off the branches, and slices the logs into lengths ready for transport. A clawed machine stacks the logs on huge trucks, using the end of a huge boom arm. The claw can swivel and pivot like the human wrist and hand, only more agile.

I had the window lowered, and the smell of cut wood and stripped pine needles filled the car. Discovering a logging operation adjacent to a pines sanctuary was like finding a butcher shop next to an animal rescue shelter. It seemed incongruous. A coyote ran across the road in front of my car, glanced our way, eyeballed the machines stripping the trees from the land, and disappeared into the woods.

The Michigan Nature Association maintains the Estivant Pines area, over 500 acres of protected land. Some of the Eastern White Pines here are hundreds of years old and average well over 100 feet tall. Trails loop through a small portion of the sanctuary, but much of it is wilderness, unmarked and swampy. Ben and I took the largest loop and walked the trail over ropey roots and thick mats of pine needles.

The first giant we came across was a ghost tree, one that had died years ago, but still stood its ground, gracefully reaching into the land with roots thicker than Ben's torso. It had a delicate twist to it, like the wind had twirled it as it grew, and that winding motion remained evident in the striations on the surface of the dead tree.

The next giant we saw was mostly hollow underneath – you could crouch inside its base (not advisable during a lightening storm, according to Grandpa Walton) – and its roots thrust deep into the ground to hold the tree in place. It was still living; only the outermost layer of a tree trunk just under the bark is alive anyway. We hugged a few trees in the largest gathering of giants, the cathedral stand. Their uppermost branches knitted together at the top, forming a woven, green canopy more than a hundred feet above us.

## Messages from the past carved in stone

Bare Bluff was the second hike I wanted to undertake on our day on the Keweenaw, but it began to rain while we were hiking the giant pines. Climbing the loose basalt hill in the rain would be tough, and I wondered if we'd be able to see much of anything when we got to the top because of the fog. A photographer that I was acquainted with, Steve Brimm, was up in Copper Harbor for the summer. He had been the one who had told me about Bare Bluff, how it was a remnant of those volcanic years eons ago.

He had said Bare Bluff was a tough climb, so I was hesitant to tackle it in the rain. "Let's go to Steve's gallery," I told Ben. "See if he's there. Maybe he'll have another suggestion for this weather."

We found his Earthworks Gallery in Copper Harbor. The little log cabin structure was open for business. We went inside and looked at the amazing photographic images covering the walls. There were many brilliant shots of Pictured Rocks, and we smiled with recognition at the spectacular sites we had so recently hiked past.

Steve migrates between North Carolina and Michigan with the weather and the smarter birds. He is a soft-spoken guy with curly hair just starting to gray and surprised eyes magnified by his large, round glasses. I introduced him to Ben and told him we had visited the giant pines. He nodded and smiled at the thought of the ancient trees.

"With this fog, I'm not sure we'd see anything from the top of Bare Bluff," I said. "I was wondering if you had any other suggestions to hike in the rain?"

"You can always hike Horseshoe Harbor. See the carvings on the stones." He looked up, searching for the word to describe them.

"Petroglyphs?"

He nodded. "That's pretty close to town."

I had a map of the area and spread it out on the counter between us. Steve traced the route with his finger.

"What's the name of the road we take a left on?" I asked.

"Doesn't have a name. What are you driving?"

I pointed to my old car parked outside.

"You can probably make it with that, if it hasn't rained too much. The road can get a little rough."

We chatted a bit more, then thanked him and headed for Horseshoe Harbor.

We drove on the no-name road until we came to a sign erected by The Nature Conservancy. We parked there and hiked a short distance through dense woods until they opened up on an otherworldly beach of rust-colored stones. The curious beach was flanked by mounded sedimentary rock formations (Copper Harbor conglomerate), more than twenty feet tall in places. All of this rock is iron-rich, tinting it reddish brown. The little bay was dotted with large mounds of the conglomerate poking out of the water, slowly being worn away by the lake.

The rock walls were easy to climb and Ben scurried up one, then along its length as it reached out into the bay. Orange and gray lichen grew on the top surface of some of the rock. Green mosses and other plants from wind-blown seeds thrived in the depressions where water gathered. Other places were devoid of any of these growths, as if the rock had recently emerged from the depths of the lake and dried in the sun. We scrambled up over one rock wall, passed through more dense forest, and emerged out onto the next little bay. Here, a shale formation was protruding from underneath the conglomerate.

Steve had told us that stromatolites – the most ancient fossilized life (ancient algae that gathered up grains of sand and rock to form a complex macro structure) – had been seen in this area. I had seen photos of stro-matolites and some samples in museums, so I knew that they could take a variety of forms, from mushroom-resembling rocks in shallow water to whitish streaks or ripples on a rock face. I took photos of many rocks while we walked, but am still not sure if we saw any of these fossilized, primitive life forms.

We hiked back to the car and drove farther along the rough road toward the tip of the Keweenaw peninsula. After powering through a few water-filled potholes, the road became impassible for my car. Muddy water filled deep holes the entire width of the road. I parked, and we began walk-ing once again.

Thimbleberries were ripening, so we picked the fuzzy, bright red berries to snack on as we walked. Wild flowers bloomed along the road; some had already transformed into their seed state, planning for next year's colorful display. We soon reached a part of the road that was submerged in deep water. We decided to return to the car, to try to find the petroglyphs we had been told were nearby.

We parked near a sandy hill and began scrambling over the rock, through bushy growth and between mature trees. The first stone carving we found resembled a Viking ship. Some scientists have dated this carving to the mid-1600s. It is of such importance that it has been protected, on site, with glass framed with metal riveted to the stone. There is some question as to who actually carved the ship. Was it done by the people on the ship itself, or by Native Americans who saw it passing on the lake? There were other carvings in the area: a bear, a "sun god" symbol (a cross within a circle), and a strange figure with the body of a man and the head of a bird. I placed my hand alongside these carvings and snapped photos, my hand giving scale to the symbols – and contrasting the living with ancient history.

It was along the shoreline of the Keweenaw Peninsula that Douglass Houghton lost his life in 1845, as did two of his traveling companions and his dog. His canoe was overturned twice in a storm while trying to reach the safety of Eagle Harbor just west of Copper Harbor. The small party was able to right their boat the first time and bail it out, but the second time it was lost. Lake Superior would hold onto Houghton's body for the winter and return it in the spring of the next year when the body washed up on the shoreline. Houghton was only 36 years old, but his contributions to the fledgling state of Michigan were immeasurable. The peninsula where he died bears his name in Houghton County and the city of Houghton. The largest inland lake in Michigan also bears his name as a tribute to this remarkable scientist and explorer.

Worn out from all the scrambling over rocky trails, Ben and I returned to our B&B to get cleaned up for dinner. One does not expect to find fine dining on the tip of this wild and remote peninsula, but we found it at the Harbor Haus in town. I am a bit of a foodie, so when the appetizer of zucchini blossoms stuffed with two kinds of cheese and various herbs arrived, I thought back to our meals on the trail – those freeze-dried morsels that swelled when hot water was dumped on them – and looked down at the beautiful plate of food.

"Ben! Stuffed zucchini blossoms!" I said, a catch in my voice.

Ben nodded at the plate of beautiful food and took one of the blossoms drizzled with a clarified butter sauce. I watched him eat just to see the pleasure spread on his face.

# Late July

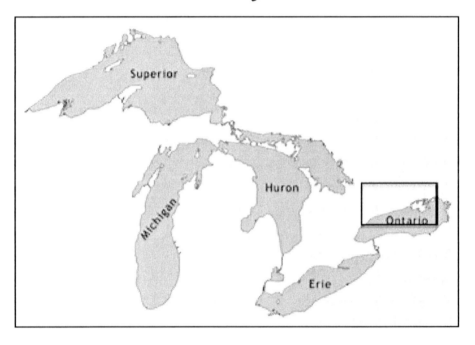

Warsaw Caves Conservation Area, "The County,"
Belleville to Toronto, Ontario;
Lake Ontario

**146 miles in 10 days**

## *Kettles* and *potholes* and *drumlins*

The Canadian Province of Ontario borders four of the Great Lakes. Only Lake Michigan is completely within America's borders. Management and conservation of the lakes is a complex task due to their vast size, but consider as well that there are eight U.S. states plus Canada bordering the lakes. Each of these entities has governments with varied viewpoints and intrinsic interests, all trying to control, propose, legislate, or otherwise affect decisions about how they will treat the waters lapping at their edges. If agreements are made between some of these shoreline keepers, but others continue to pollute or abuse the lakes, it is difficult to effectively conserve these waters.

The Great Lakes Water Compact (which concerns the usage of the water in the Great Lakes Basin) was the first piece of legislation fully endorsed by all lakeshore governments.

Since Canada has almost as much Great Lakes shoreline as the U.S., I thought it important to explore how Canadians are interacting with the lakes. This was one of the big goals I had set for this hike. Indeed, my time on Lake Ontario would take place entirely in Canada, and I was looking forward with great anticipation to this part of my journey along the fifth and final Great Lake in my adventure.

I would begin in the city of Belleville – which happens to be the birthplace of Herbert Henry Dow, the founder of Dow Chemical – then hike west to Toronto. In addition, there were two areas in particular I wanted to explore by doing day hikes in Ontario. One is a bit inland from the lake, a place called the Warsaw Caves Conservation Area. The other is on a large peninsula reaching into the lake, the Sandbanks Provincial Park. Both of these areas have been marked with distinction by these flowing waters and shaped by the hard hand of the glaciers.

When the last of the glaciers retreated around ten thousand years ago, the lakes were much larger than they are today. They were overflowing with water from the melting ice sheets. The lakes continued to ebb and flow for thousands of years. It is only in the last few thousand that the lakes have settled within the general shoreline where they are today, during which time the overall basin began to drain the way it currently flows.

At first, shortly after the retreat of the glaciers, the lakes were unsettled. They raged and calmed, flowed at first in one direction, then another. The upper lakes flowed to the north for a while since the immense weight of the glaciers had depressed the land, tilting it, tipping the entire region to the north.

As this land rebounded (it is still rebounding even today), water began flowing to the southeast. For many years, prehistoric Lake Algonquin (now Lake Huron) flowed east into prehistoric Lake Iroquois (now Lake Ontario), bypassing the Lake Erie basin entirely. This watery connection was called the Kirkfield Spillway. Scientists theorize that there was a massive ice dam that held back the water for a time. When the dam broke, a wall of water exploded through the region. This raging river scoured and shaped the land in ways that are still evident today, and I wanted to see it for myself.

I drove east across the state of Michigan, and paid the toll to cross the Blue Water Bridge in Port Huron. At this point, almost 700 miles of my adventure were behind me. As I looked down from the bridge onto the waters of Lake Huron funneling into the St. Clair River, I thought back to the beginning of my hike, those cool and windy April days when I passed underneath this very bridge and walked on around the edge of Michigan's thumb during the first part of my journey. Now, I felt as if I was crossing paths with my former self, and I tossed a little wave to her as she headed north carrying her white backpack.

I took the 401 east, then picked up 402 to get me through Toronto. Near the town of Clarington, I headed northeast toward the Warsaw Caves Conservation Area.

Water can wear away rock, given enough time. But it is especially good at dissolving limestone. Most caves are formed in limestone deposits where the rock has been slowly eaten away by water. In this conservation area, there are a series of caves that you can crawl into. The entire area has a cap of limestone, and as the waters raged through here, they blasted into fissures in the stone, reaching underneath rocks and churning out caves. Today, the caves are marked along the trail that runs above the ground. Some of the caves had ropes that reached down into them to aid hikers who wished to spelunk a bit.

That was not me. I had several reasons for not entering any of these subterranean caves:

1. I was hiking alone.
2. I don't enter any cave that you have to "wriggle into."
3. I saw that James Franco movie where he had to saw off his own arm.

The take-away message from that Franco movie for me: *Always carry a really good knife in case you have to saw off your arm.* Having to perform surgery on yourself is horrible enough without having to use a crappy knife.

Yes, I poked my head in a couple of the caves, pushed my camera through a few narrow openings and took some flash photos. But I didn't wriggle underground anywhere.

And yes, I still have both my arms.

Hiking through the area was fascinating because the limestone blocks on the surface had shifted and tilted. They had fractured and moved as the river shaped them, while it was carving out voids beneath the surface. Trees poked up between the rocks, and pine needles littered the path. Some trees had to reach over the rocks, creating a beautiful, worn webbing of roots on the surface of the weathered limestone.

It was in this area that I saw my first *potholes* or *kettles*. These are glacial features, holes or depressions formed as the glaciers receded. Some larger ones were formed as buried blocks of ice held space in piles of rock debris; when those ice-blocks eventually melted, the surface collapsed down to form a distinctive kettle bowl. But the most interesting kettles were actually drilled in the rock by whirlpools or eddies in the swift-moving river. Sometimes these swirling waters would take ahold of small rocks, captured in a little depression, and spin them around and around against the surface of the limestone, making a smooth hole, going deeper and deeper like a drill. The first holes I came across ranged in size from finger width to large enough to plunge my fist into. Many of them were more than a foot deep, too.

At the end of the caves trail, I came across part of the Indian River that winds through the park. This waterway is a placid, gentle remnant of the waters that once raged here. This river has the odd habit of disappearing. In places it vanishes from sight to course underneath the limestone boulders in voids created thousands of years ago. There were several places along the trail where I could hear the river gurgling beneath the rocks I was walking on.

I hiked the Kettle and Lookout Trail next to see the largest kettles in the park. The first one I saw was so large I could have curled up inside the depression. My favorite kettle was toward the end of the trail, a hole drilled completely through the rock ledge so that I could see through the bottom. It was so large I could have slid down into it and out the far end of the hole. I sat on the edge and dangled my feet into the void. The walls of the kettle were smooth and rounded, the hole generally conical, wider at the top and narrowing toward the bottom.

For a kettle of this size to form, there must have been a long-term whirlpool here spinning and spinning, using any loose rock or even sand particles to scour away to create this formation. I ran my hand along the smooth walls and over the cracks in the limestone layers. I sat there a long while looking at the strange terrain. With all the places to hide within the rock, all the twists and turns to the trail, I kept a lookout for any hobbit that might pop out and wave to me. They are, I've heard, a friendly people.

On the drive south to Belleville, I had to zigzag to cross all the waterways in the area, more remnants of the water that once filled this region. The hand of the glacier was also evident on the land. *Drumlins,* elongated hills formed of glacial till, point in the direction of glacial retreat. Now goats and cows grazed on lush grasses, and the corn reached for the sky.

## Let's go to The County!

I wanted to do one more day-hike before walking the edge of Lake Ontario to Toronto. Just south of Belleville across the Bay of Quinte is a large land-mass reaching into the lake. It was a peninsula until the Murray Canal sliced its connection to the mainland. This is Prince Edward County, and Canadians refer to it fondly as "The County" as in, "I vacationed in The County." The County is irregularly shaped with many lobes reaching in various directions into the lake, giving it over three hundred miles of shore-line. And much of that shoreline is sandy beach and bay-mouth dunes.

While exploring The County, I wound my way through the many vine-yards and stopped to look at a lavender farm. I noticed that there were many solar arrays erected on private land. The reason is simple: Ontario has committed to shutting down or converting its remaining coal-fired elec-tricity plants no later than 2014 and to increase power created from green sources. Accordingly, the province has an initiative that offers a 20-year contract to buy solar-produced electricity from private landowners at a rate that ensures the owners recoup their investment within the first decade. Ontario has also pushed to increase electricity produced by wind; it is now the leading province in this regard.

There are a couple of tiny towns in The County, and I drove to one called Wellington to walk the beach there. Small stones were scattered over sand, and broken rock chunks rested underneath the waves. The dune for-mations here are actually a huge sandbar about five miles in length that formed on top of the bedrock. The long sandbar isolates the interior West

Lake from Lake Ontario. It used to seal it off completely until a channel was cut for boats to access the West Lake near Wellington. This area has a strong fishing history. A sign on the beach told the tale of one epic night in 1857 when fishermen worked all night at that spot, hauling in their nets and casting them out again, time after time, until dawn broke. In the morning, it was estimated that 40,000 whitefish had been gathered from the lake in a single night.

I drove to the other side of West Lake and joined a line of cars waiting to enter Sandbanks Provincial Park. Many of the vehicles had license plates from Quebec, and, as I walked the dunes later, I would hear as much French spoken as English. Canadians flock to this sandy park for their summer vacations. I hiked on trails through the dunes and then returned to the beach. The shoreline was deserted at the far end of my walk, but as I headed back, I encountered more and more people enjoying the warm summer day.

I drove through the center of The County to the city of Picton, then made my way to see one of the most geologically puzzling features there: the Lake on the Mountain. This pristine lake is elevated 150 feet above Lake Ontario, yet is within sight of the Great Lake. It is fed by multiple springs and is over a hundred feet deep. This little lake has given rise to many legends, and it was revered by First Nations people in the region who would travel there to leave offerings to the spirits of the lake.

The way the lake was formed is still under debate by geologists. Theories vary from it being drilled by a huge whirlpool in a glacial fissure (similar to how kettles were formed) to a meteorite crashing there forming the depression to the more simple theory that water wore through the limestone base of an earlier depression, which then collapsed, forming the much larger and deeper lake that is there today. Even if visitors know nothing of this history and geology, the Lake on the Mountain still fascinates.

## The most loyal Loyalists

I took the ferry back to the mainland, then drove east a bit to explore parts of the area's lakeshore I didn't have time to walk. While in The County, I had seen the first signs for the Loyalist Parkway and wondered what that was all about. Turns out that those American Colonists who chose to stay loyal to Britain during the Revolutionary War were not treated very well after America won its independence. Most modern Americans think that the early colonies united as one and rose up en masse against British rule, but fully a third of the colonists wanted to remain a British colony. A third wanted independence. And a third were too busy clearing land, putting up food for the winter, and were possibly preoccupied with a toothache or some ailment to have much of an opinion on the revolutionary matter.

Of the third that were against the war, about half of them openly opposed it – they were called loyalists – and the most vocal were persecuted after the fighting was over. Loyalists were hit with high taxes, sometimes their land and possessions were seized, and individuals were often tarred and feathered and even imprisoned.

Facing that treatment at the hands of their neighbors and the new government, many chose to flee north to British-held Canada. Many of these Loyalists went on to establish new settlements along Lake Ontario's northern shores.

If I tell you they fled by boat, you might imagine them getting onto a comfortable steamship with their trunks full of possessions, looking pensively out through the glass windows of their cabins as the boat powered them to the north. Not so. In many cases, they tossed what little they could carry into the bottom of a long rowboat and fled across rough waters, praying to not drown before they made landfall.

While touring The County and the area between there and the city of Kingston at the east end of Lake Ontario where begins to flow into the St. Lawrence River, I saw many tributes to the bravery and loyalty to the British Crown of the few hundred souls that fled one country to help settle another. The place where the ferry landed on the mainland – a town called Adolphus – was the first place the Loyalists settled in 1784.

There is a monument and cemetery there. I walked around the walled cemetery. I calculated that some of the individuals lived to a ripe old age: 64 years, 58 years. Others died as infants or toddlers. There was a display with a replica of the type of boat they traveled in, an open bateau, near the water. This flat-bottomed rowboat looked sturdy, but I would not want to be caught in a storm in the middle of the lake in it.

I stopped at a chip truck in a park along the Loyalist Parkway. The owner, an elderly man with a fully gray beard, was peeling softball-size potatoes outside the truck as I approached. He finished expertly stripping the peel from the potato in his hand with a sharp paring knife, then dropped it into the five-gallon pail of water to join the other starchy balls deftly liberated from their skins. Then he went inside the truck to wait on me through the window. I glanced at the menu, noticing a hand-written sign for the Loyalist Special: a brat, hand-cut fries, and a drink.

Perfect.

If you want to experience Canada's connection to their British heritage, get chips (fries) from a chip truck. No one does chips like the British. When done properly, a hand-cut potato will be deep fried at two different temperatures, the first to cook the potato, the second, higher temperature to crisp the outside. These chip trucks maintain this art at roadside places where tourists stop. They also believe in putting out malted vinegar to sprinkle on the fries, a taste treat not often recognized in the states.

While most Americans kind of shrugged at the 200th anniversary of The War of 1812 (which largely went unnoticed in much of the country) it was a much bigger deal in Canada. During the war, the Americans repeatedly invaded Canadian territory. Thomas Jefferson advocated these incursions; he thought it would be easy to take the region from the British.

He was wrong about that. The Americans never held Canadian territory for long. Still, the early settlers in Canada considered these incursions a huge threat. The Loyalists – those former Colonists who now called Canada their home – were among the most fervent in the defense of their land and are celebrated as heroes, not only for founding many communities there, but also for defending their new homeland during The War of 1812.

## Squishy boots & Tim Hortons

The next day I set out from the lovely Montrose Inn B&B in Belleville (modeled, oddly enough, after the Governor's mansion in Atlanta, Georgia) and began walking west toward Toronto. A gentle sprinkle evolved into torrential rain that first morning, bringing the land snails out of hiding to slither about on the roadside grasses. Their gently swirled shells were outlined with brown stripes that followed the curve of their snail houses. I snapped a few photos of these mobile roadside decorations before the rain came down in sheets, and I had to store my camera away, quickly pull on my rain pants over my hiking pants, and fit a garbage bag over my backpack.

The rain came so fast that it flooded the surface of the road. Passing cars lofted waves of water my way as they plowed through the floods. After taking a couple of waves on my back, I hiked down the slope of the road-side ditch and up the other side to distance myself from the deluge.

One of the nicest features of Canada, in my opinion as a hiker, is the chain of donut restaurants called Tim Hortons. As I hiked past the Royal Air Force Base in Trenton in the pounding rain, I hoped there would be a Tim Hortons – Canadians often refer to the chain affectionately as "Timmy's" – to be found in the city. And, sure enough, there it was, just as Canadian law apparently mandated. I ducked inside dripping wet and waited out the storm with a cup of coffee and a couple of donuts.

A crueler and a chocolate-frosted Boston cream, if you must know.

When the rain subsided, I hiked to the Murray Canal that slices The County from the mainland and began hiking its length on a dirt road that was marked with signs as "unmaintained." Ontario has established a Waterfront Trail that runs from Montreal to the city of Niagara-on-the-Lake. It stitches together mostly roadways with some trails and paths. Route 2 between Belleville and Trenton was part of the trail, and so was the little, unmaintained dirt road threading between the canal and a lush wetland.

The water-filled potholes were easy to hike around at first, but then they took up the entire width of the narrow road. With no way to skirt them, I began walking through the middle of puddle after puddle. As they got deeper, water soon filled my boots, and I was often up to mid-shin in muddy water. My boots were pretty soaked from the rain and car waves from earlier in the day, so I kept slogging along until I reached the far end of the canal and arrived at the bridge that would allow me to cross over and make my way to my next B&B near the shores of Lake Ontario.

I picked up a newspaper in the lobby and squished my way to my room for the night. I pulled off my soaked boots, pulled out the soggy insoles, and stuffed them tight with newspaper to draw out the water. It poured again that evening. The entire region – most of America, too – had been in a drought up to that point, so I did not begrudge the land the rain.

## A turtle parade on the *tombolo*

In the morning, I went to the lake's edge and looked across the water to the Presqu'ile Provincial Park and the bright white lighthouse there. This entire park – and much of the area where I would walk near the lakeshore – had been submerged for several thousand years after the glaciers retreated.

Ancient Lake Iroquois was much larger than the present-day Lake Ontario. Much of the route I had already walked was within sight of the lake, but elevated from lake level. In many places the land stepped down to the lake, each step marking an earlier edge of a once-upon-a-time lakeshore, an ancient beach left stranded as the waters shrank to evolve into today's Lake Ontario.

Presqu'ile used to be an island, but over time a complex sand-bar formation called a *tombolo* formed, linking it to the mainland as a peninsula. These finger-like formations are still evident in the park, and lush wetlands thrive in the spaces between them, creating excellent and varied habitat for wildlife. I walked the northern edge of the park where it had attached itself to the mainland. I noticed the many "Turtle Crossing" signs along the roads.

It was a hot day, so I soon was hoping for a store to appear along the way, a place where I could buy a cold drink or maybe even some ice cream. My filtering bottle assured that I would never be without water, but when I was dipping it in a lukewarm lake, it wasn't the most refreshing beverage.

On a curve in the road near the water I came upon a small store, but it looked closed. As I got closer, I noticed a small pick-up truck parked to the side. The truck's radio was on, the windows rolled down to let the music spill out. I crossed the narrow road, and a large man in his 50s zoomed out to meet me in the parking area on his motorized mobility scooter.

"Are you hiking the trail?" he asked, braking to a stop in the middle of the paved area.

"All the way to Toronto."

"I've seen thousands of bikes since they established the trail, but you're the first hiker."

The man's name was Randy, and he launched into the history of the park and the trail, barely taking a breath between topics. I was getting a little woozy standing there in the sunshine with the heat radiating from the pavement, and I glanced around for some shade or any clue that the store was open while I waited for an opening in Randy's recitation.

Finally, I managed to break into his story.

"Is the store open? I'd like to get something to drink."

"Oh, sure, sure," he said, as he maneuvered his scooter in a neat arc to lead me back to a shed where the truck was parked. It turned out that Randy was manning the store; he just preferred to hang out in the parking lot.

"The owner keeps a small fridge in the shed." Randy pointed to the battered shed attached to the battered store that now, on closer assessment, I could see was stuffed with used things to resell.

"I can't get in there, but you can." Randy pointed from his scooter seat to the shed, at an unlocked padlock hanging from a metal loop and strap closure. Old wood was piled up around the shed, and the whole place was starting to seem a little dicey, except that Randy was obviously a nice guy stuck on his scooter and starved for conversation.

After pulling two cold drinks out of the tiny fridge and paying Randy, I watched him as he maneuvered to the space between his truck and a tall hedge with a narrow gap in it. "Go through there and grab a chair," he said. "Then you can sit in the breeze."

Now, the day was incredibly still, so I wasn't sure what "breeze" he was talking about. But when I went through the gap, to my surprise, the air was indeed moving. I grabbed a chair, and he nimbly backed his scooter to give me a space. It seems that the tiny movement of air over the lake was somehow funneled to this one spot and accelerating through the gap in the hedge. I sat there, amazed to feel the cool air moving across my back that was soaked with sweat from carrying my pack.

"A great breeze you've got here. Thanks," I said. I settled in to hear Randy's stories. He told me about the turtles coming up out of the wetlands by the hundreds and crossing the road. How he sometimes drove his scooter along the road at night with a flashlight to watch them dig their holes and lay their eggs. He said that the snappers come all at once in a parade, like someone had given them a signal.

Whatever he wanted to tell me was fine. I was happy to sit and listen and enjoy the cool flowing air.

## Limestone and a good marriage

At the Loughbreeze Bay B&B where I stayed the next night, I could look out the backyard, back across the lake, and see the west side of Presqu'ile across the water. This B&B had an unusual neighbor: a limestone quarry so close that when they blasted to free up the stone, the house shook beneath our feet.

"Do you want a tour of the mine?" Frances, the owner of the B&B,

asked me. "I can call over there to let them know we're coming."

I never decline a mine tour.

A spritely woman with bright white hair, Frances jumped up and ran into the house to make the call. After hiking all day, I was less nimble.

In a couple moments, she came back out onto the deck. "We can go over anytime."

"Let her finish her water, Beauty," Lawrence, her husband, said to her.

Lawrence had an assortment of endearments he called Frances. I don't think I ever heard him use her name. We chatted some more, and Frances proudly told me that she was descended from Loyalists who settled this lakeshore.

After I had drained my water bottle, Frances asked, "Ready to go?"

I nodded and slowly stood. My muscles were pretty well toned by this point in my adventure, but I had hiked 18 miles this day (and 16 soggy ones the day before), so things tended to tighten up after I sat a bit. Frances led me to the driveway, and as I wondered which vehicle we were going to take, she began walking on the road back toward the mine. It was to be a walking tour, and Frances kept a brisk pace.

We hiked the road into the mine entrance, through the gate with the Holcim Mine sign, past the warnings about blasting going on that day. I ask about the warning sign in the middle of the road.

"Oh, they're done blasting for the day," Frances said. She leads me along the road for a bit, then heads off on a side path and scrambles up a tall embankment. At the top, we look down into the mine. There are several neat, rectangular cutouts in the stone-slab expanse of more than 600 acres where they had methodically removed the stone. The top edges of the walls are drilled with evenly spaced holes ready for the next round of charges that would be dropped in to blast away the next section of rock wall.

The recent rain had pooled into a string of connected ponds at the bottom of the depressions. I look for something to snap the scene to scale and saw a front loader in the distance. After visiting the Calcite mine in Rogers City, I knew that these pieces of machinery may look small in the scene, but the bucket on the loader was probably tall enough for me to stand inside with my arms raised above my head and still I wouldn't be able to touch the top.

"I know limestone is used for many things," I said, "like steel production. And to clean up emissions from coal-fired plants. So what is the limestone here used for?"

"Cement. It all goes to Mississauga to the cement plant."

"All of it?"

"Yes. The limestone is the perfect composition for making strong cement. There is one ship that makes a constant loop between the mine and the plant."

We headed back to the road and walked deeper into the mine's land.

"So you just call over when you want to walk around here?" I asked, amazed.

"I'm on the board that helps the community interface with the mine, so they all know me. Are you okay to hop over this gate?" she asked as we approach a chained gate across a two-track.

I watched her nimbly climb up and over the gate, and found myself thinking that maybe America has missed out on some great genetic traits lost in the Loyalist emigration if this woman in her 60s could so gracefully climb over a four-foot gate.

I chuckled as I stiffly follow her over, trying to keep up as we head out to the lakeshore.

Limestone mines are pretty simple, conceptually: blast the wall of the mine to loosen the rock, load rock into trucks, dump rock into a crusher, sort the size of rock if you want to get fancy like at the Calcite mine, load crushed rock onto ships for transport to industry. This mine has a conveyor system that took the rock out to a dock constructed in the lake a bit, far enough out that the water deepened enough to allow the huge ship, the *James Norris,* to snuggle up against cement-filled metal rings driven into the lakebed.

The boat was docked as we approached the water's edge. I could see one of the arms of the conveyor spilling crushed limestone into the middle hold of the boat.

I pulled out my camera.

"Put your camera away," Frances said.

"Okay." I was startled by the serious tone of her voice, and I palmed the little camera.

"Security is tight here. They are most certainly watching us."

"Security?"

"This ship sometimes travels in U.S. waters, so it's under your Homeland

Security rules. If we hadn't called to get permission to be on their beach, we would have been greeted by security by now."

I hadn't seen a single person since we entered the mine's property, so this seemed implausible.

"Oh, they know me. They see my white hair and my glasses and they know it's me, but they'll come out to greet even me if I don't call over for permission first." She looked at the expression on my face. "They gave me a tour of that ship not too long ago. Standing on the bridge, you can look up and down the shore and see everything, like it's being magnified many times."

We walked back to the house along the water's edge for a bit. There is a sandy beach that is off limits to the public because of the mine. There are warning signs posted, prohibiting even landing a boat on this shore. When we were near the point, Frances tells me it is now okay to take photos if I wanted, so I snapped a few looking back across the water.

Later, when I researched the mine, I was shocked to see many photos posted online by the mine itself. So much for security.

Frances and Lawrence insisted I eat dinner with them, and when I smelled the chicken they were roasting, I could not formulate any argument for eating the freeze-dried food in my pack. I accepted their offer.

The chicken was accompanied by fresh beans and beets from their garden. We had a wonderful dinner in the backyard with Lake Ontario lapping at the edges of their land. Frances, as she had told me, was descended from Loyalists who settled the region. Lawrence is American by birth and had lived in Canada for over a decade. We talked about the Great Lakes and the two countries bordering them. Frances told me that she had spent some summers living on Canada's northern shore of Lake Erie when she was young.

"Lake Erie was in horrible shape," she told me. "We would hold our noses because of the smell, and run through all the black gunk near the shore to get out to water that was clearer for swimming."

There was little industry on the northern shore of Lake Erie at the time. All of that pollution had to come from elsewhere, from upstream – Detroit, and farther upstream from that – and from Cleveland across the lake.

There were tall, black locust trees growing at the edges of their property near the water. The bark of this tree is craggy and deeply furrowed. I had seen some ancient specimens of this tree along my Lake Ontario hike so far, and had stopped several times to take photos of their gracefully curving forms.

"You've got a lovely spot here," I told them as I gazed across the calm water to Presqu'ile Park that I had passed during that day's hike. I pointed at their trees. "I saw some huge black locust along the hike today. I'm surprised they survived the lumbering phase."

"You know why that is?" Lawrence asked. "See how they twist and curve? They really move in the wind . . ."

". . . and that messes with the grain of the wood," Frances finished.

"The wood is strong – like iron to cut through," Lawrence continued.

"But the grain is messed up, so they couldn't use them," Frances concluded.

The flow of conversation was easy, and they often finished each other's thoughts. They never talked over each other, but seemed to have a separate way of communicating in the airwaves between them, picking up on their spouse's need of a fact and filling it in gracefully, or tag-teaming a story – not competitively, but as a way of telling it better, sharing the experience again as they told it.

This is one of the hallmarks of a good marriage, I thought, this cooperative conversation.

The next day I was sent off with a huge breakfast and a bag of fresh green beans to munch along the way. I planned to walk to the city of Cobourg. This mapped out at over 20 miles, so I cut through some fields and briefly walked along a train track to slice off a bit of the mileage.

I don't suggest hiking on railroad tracks – especially in Canada where they have commuter trains that periodically zip along – but it was going to be another hot day, and slicing at an angle across the land instead of making squared corners along the roads was enticing. Much of the land between the waterfront trail road and the lake here is agricultural – toasted hayfields shorn of their first cutting, pasture for cows, some orchards heavy with ripening fruit.

Lake Ontario glimmered in the near distance, just past the bucolic scenery.

## Lemon shortbread

About a mile before I reached a public beach access where I could refill my water bottle, I came across a roadside farm with a little stand. I thought they would just sell ordinary produce, but as I approached, I saw that their produce was organic. They also sold things like artisanal goat cheese, herb-infused olive oils, and – could it be? – lemon shortbread cookies in clear bags tied with bright ribbon.

Now, I'm a chocolate cookie person by nature (choc chip, choc oatmeal, choc-choc!), but on this steamy Canadian day, nothing seemed more appealing than these perfectly formed shortbread cookies, sporting their little curls of lemon zest. I cradled a package of them while waiting in line.

Yes, a line of people were queuing up, stopping by to take advantage of the fine offerings and chat with the owner about this year's crop and their community. Many people seemed to be regular vacationers to the area. They conversed about opening up their cabins and how many weeks they would be there. When I saw the owner open a small fridge, I wondered if they might have bottled water. It's not that I didn't like drinking out of the lake, I just didn't like having to drink warm water on a hot day. When it was my turn, I paid for the cookies and asked if they had bottled water.

"No," the owner said, a narrow, sun-kissed man in his 50s. "But you can go behind the house to the outdoor kitchen there and fill up. The water is excellent and fully potable."

I went behind the house and turned on the tap at the sink there. There was an outdoor gas range set into the tiled counter next to the sink, and the entire patio area was in the shade of tall trees, adjacent to a pond. What a brilliant idea to put the kitchen outside, especially if you were going to can things in the heat of the summer when everything ripened.

I dumped the hot water from my bottle and filled up from the tap. Then I cupped my hands and drank from the cold, rushing water. I wet my bandana, tied it dripping around my neck, and continued on my hike.

I stopped at the nearby beach to have a snack. The cirrus clouds had smeared and merged across the light blue sky, masking it mostly white. A few sailboats dotted the placid water, and two men paddled a canoe parallel to the shore. The beach was strewn with a layer of tumbled stones.

Finding a shady spot underneath a tree that had been partially knocked down onto the beach, I sat and pulled out my green beans, my lemon cookies, and my cold bottle of water and enjoyed a little summertime feast.

The temperature had been bumping up against 80 degrees ever since I began this leg of the hike. This afternoon it got above 80, and the high clouds dissolved so that the sun beat down on me, unimpeded. As I was making my way up an incline on the road arching over railroad tracks, a van pulled over near me.

Lawrence was at the wheel, and Frances jumped out the other side.

"Hello!" I said, a bit surprised.

"We forgot to give you this," Frances said, as she held out an apple and a bottle of water.

"Thank you!" I said.

As I took them from her, I realized that the bottle of water was frozen solid. Holding it to the side of my hot face, I let out a long sigh. "Oh, that's lovely."

"We were coming into Cobourg, so we thought we'd track you down." She jumped into the van and they sped off.

Before I resumed walking, I positioned the ice bottle so it rode between my neck and my pack, pressing its coolness onto the base of my neck. I think I even heard a sigh of relief from my backpack.

Cobourg is another town that was settled by Loyalists, so it has a rich history. It is also the largest city in Northumberland County, a harbor town cobbled together from a group of smaller villages. One of the villages was called Hardscrabble, and I thought they had lost something when they stopped using that descriptive name.

Cobourg has many historic buildings with identification plaques out front, boasting some fine stone buildings built in the 1800s. I strolled through town and found a café with outside seating. When I finally made it to the hotel, my destination, I was pretty done in for the day.

The clerk at the desk informed me that they were booked solid, as were all hotels in town due to several weddings and a triathlon. Not a room to be had.

The next town, Port Hope, was only five miles away, but I had already walked twenty miles in the heat. I called a B&B there and found out that they had a room. Best of all, the owner was in Cobourg and would stop by and get me before returning home.

Like Cobourg, the city of Port Hope has lovingly preserved many historic buildings there, sitting serenely on the banks of the Ganaraska River.

The next morning, I tied ice cubes into my bandana before securing it around my neck. It was going to be a broiling day again. I headed out of town and found my way onto the most scenic stretch of the Waterfront Trail that I would walk, stretching from Port Hope to Bowmanville.

The trail is a narrow road most of the way. It winds through some beautiful country with rolling hills and farms, small creeks and tiny towns. The lake is often within sight, but the land between the road and water is privately held. Signs often reminded me of the Canadian right to own right up to the water's edge.

In a tall stand of blooming thistle, a small flock of monarch butterflies circled and landed to feast, flitting around to find a better drink of nectar. Morning glories lifted their round faces to the bright sunlight, and Queen Anne's lace grew tall along the roadside. It seemed to be an exceptional year for that lacey flower. Some of the intricate, circled blooms were wider than my hand.

I did encounter some industry along the way, power plants and such, but they were usually tucked along the water, a bit away from the path where I was walking.

Bicyclists love this stretch of road, and several hundred passed me that day. Many of them were cycling from Toronto to Montreal in three days as part of a group tour. Near midday, a procession of Model-Ts drove by, occasionally sneaking up on me and sounding their *a-ooga* horns, scaring the hell out of me.

Toward the end of the day, I was getting hungry. But after walking in the heat, the last thing I wanted to eat was something dry or dehydrated, which was all I carried in my pack, so I kept pressing on toward the hotel. The trail became a paved path for a stretch that passed through a cornfield. The corn was immature and stunted near the path.

I looked around and, sure the coast was clear, snatched one small ear of corn that wouldn't have time to mature before harvest. I shucked it and ate it raw. The tiny kernels were still pointy since they hadn't had time and moisture to disengage from the silk strand. I ate it down to the cob and sucked the cob for every last drop of moisture. It was fantastic.

I had to wander a bit at the end of the day. The trail wasn't marked clearly, and roads that my GPS promised would continue did not. They abruptly stopped at the edge of mucky fields or forests. The warnings against trespassing convinced me to hike extra miles in big squared-off, roady chunks.

As the sun descended through the clouds, the rays were diffused and streaked out toward the land. At one point, the rays illuminated the black smoke in the air from the industry along the lake. By the time I got to the hotel, I had hiked the longest day of this adventure, the longest day ever in my life, 27 miles.

I took it easy the next day, hiking only 14 miles to the west side of the city of Oshawa. Every step brought me closer to Toronto, and the lakeshore became increasingly developed. Most of this day, the trail stayed between railroad tracks and highway 401; high-voltage towers marched in this space, too, since the Darlington Nuclear plant sits along the shore here.

Astonishingly, the trail curves through the buffer zone around the nuclear plant. A narrow pedestrian corridor allows people to squeeze through the barbed wire-topped fence there. Some of the land was planted with corn, but most was lush with weeds and occasional trees. Ponds were filled with ducks and swans, and a sentinel, great blue heron. In one pond, nine painted turtles balanced along a thin limb at the surface of the water. Many of them held on to the turtle closest to them to form a festive turtle conga line.

The trail emerged from the natural portion and dumped me onto a side road where a new sewage treatment plant was under construction. About a decade ago, Ontario set aside C$2.5 billion to improve the province's ability to keep raw sewage from entering the lake. Some of these funds were used to establish water-filtering wetlands. One, near Presqu'ile, even had a stretch of elevated boardwalk where people could gather and watch birds.

One of the biggest complications in treating raw sewage is when large amounts of runoff from storms flood into the treatment plant, overwhelming its capacity. These are the conditions under which treatment plants may have to release untreated sewage into rivers and lakes. One way to get around this is to create retention ponds or wetlands that can capture rain runoff from streets. If this runoff is held for a time in a healthy wetland, the water is naturally cleansed before it makes its way to the lake.

Many major cities around the Great Lakes are installing such wetlands to provide this function. Some cities, like Detroit, have installed holding plants for combined runoff/sewage so it can be at least partially treated before being released. In new developments, street runoff is often segregated from sewage mains, but it is difficult and costly to try to retrofit an established city burdened with the older type of system that combines the two.

One doesn't often make time to contemplate sewage. The hike toward Toronto, seeing the small towns and farmland giving way to industry and power plants, approaching the second-largest city on the Great Lakes, was a visual representation of the increasingly complex interaction people have with the land and the water. I was acutely aware of the obvious toll taken on both as population density increases.


## The fattest of lips

After hiking through a lovely provincial park, the trail took me to the Canadian Headquarters for General Motors. The rounded entryway to the building was wrapped in a billboard-size photo of the newest Cadillac model. Yes, there was quite a variety of things to see along the Waterfront Trail! The trail is designated along the curved drive that passes by the front doors of GM's building, then it winds through a wildlife preserve that sits just past it.

Toward the end of this day, I realized that my lips were swollen. The bottom one, especially. They had gotten sunburned the day before. By the end of the day, my bottom lip was about twice its normal size, and I found myself tucking it underneath my top lip to get it out of the sun.

Since the next day's hike would have taken me past another nuclear power plant, I shouldered my pack and took a short hop on the commuter train, to avoid repeating that not-so-pleasant experience. I figured there were only so many nuclear plants and high-voltage power lines one should walk near in a lifetime, and I had reached my limit.

The trail continued through Pickering, staying close to the water for longer stretches and crossing over Ontario's Rouge River. As I hiked into the town of Scarborough, the clouds gathered overhead, darkened, and let loose fat droplets. I ducked into a sandwich shop and took a window seat to watch the storm rip through the area. It got so dark that drivers – if they dared to continue through the sheeting rain – turned on their headlights in mid-day.

Winds whipped the tops of the trees around in circles, ripping off loose branches. I ate a sandwich and relaxed while people struggled with umbrellas or ran from their car into the restaurant. When the rain let up, I pulled up my hood and hiked the remaining miles of the day, then iced my big, fat lip at the hotel.

There is a tall bluff at the lakeshore as you approach Toronto. Spots on the map with names like Cliffcrest and Cliffside hint at this. This formation is east of the Niagara Escarpment and is earthen rather than stone. It stretches for almost 9 miles along the shore and is over 200 feet tall at its highest point.

Overlooking the lake on the bluff is St. Augustine's Seminary, which has allowed the Waterfront Trail to pass through their land. The main brick building of the seminary is capped with a cross-topped cupola, sheathed in metal that has oxidized and weathered to a pleasing, green patina. The middle third of the cupola is all windows, allowing light to pass through and the blue of the sky to color the middle of the structure. The brick building looks industrial, or maybe like a prison from the 1950s, but this topper is all grace and style. I found myself looking back over my shoulder to study it for as long as I could still see it through the trees.

The descent to lake level was sometimes abrupt, as it proved to be on my route that led through Bluffer's Park. The trail passes through parks and neighborhoods, on the road near Toronto's water intake, and then through the sprawling beachy parks on the southeast side of the city. The Kew-Balmy Beach in Toronto was sprinkled with people even at mid-day on a Wednesday. People walked the boardwalk or sat on the beach. Many swam in the lake, although I wondered about the water quality so near the city. Then I saw a sign along the boardwalk noting this beach had been awarded the Blue Flag Status for good water quality and environmental management and education. Go Toronto!

The clean status of the beach and water is remarkable when you consider that Lake Ontario is the most downstream lake of the Great Lakes, accepting water that was recently in Lake Erie before plunging over Niagara Falls to reach Lake Ontario. The water stays in Lake Ontario for a mean length of time of six years before exiting through the St. Lawrence River and scooting out to the North Atlantic Ocean.

I caught my first glimpse of Toronto's CN Tower while on the boardwalk at Kew-Balmy Beach. For me, it meant that the end of this portion of the hike was near enough to see. The trail continued around Toronto's main water-treatment plant and the port. Much of this land was fenced off, but there were occasional, intentional doorways for small animals wishing to enter the wild land on the other side.

## "C'est carachidebile!"

I made my way into the heart of the city and walked by the Hockey Hall of Fame (or, as I was informed, *Le Temple De La Renommee Du Hockey!* in French) and to the completion of this part of my hike at the Royal York Hotel. This is one of a series of grand hotels built by the Canadian Pacific Railway in key locations near their railroad tracks all across Canada. The hotel was the tallest building in Toronto when opened back in 1929.

The next morning, the sun rose behind nearby Union Station, making all the windows glow as the burnt orange and yellow light passed through the grand edifice.

At the station, I bought some candy bars for the train ride that would take me back to my car that I had left back in Belleville where I began this Lake Ontario portion of my journey. When traveling to another country, I always sample their chocolate, everything from high-end chocolatier truffles to lowly candy bars. While you might think Canada would have the same candy as America, given the close proximity of the two countries, I discover the country has some distinctive offerings.

My favorite had become the Coffee Crisp bar, a layered wafer infused with coffee flavor and dipped in something resembling milk chocolate. It delivers a wonderful one-two punch: the coffee hit plus the chocolate hit. There is also the Wunderbar (the German word for marvelous). It promises a "peanut butter caramel experience." Oddly, the word "Wunderbar" had a horned, Viking hat emblem on its top. That confused me. I got even more confused by the taste, like a Butterfinger had been crossed with a Twix.

One thing I love about Canada is that they gently manage to teach you a bit of French during your visit. The exit? Well, it's right over there, clearly labeled both "exit" and "sortie." There you go, you just learned the French word for exit. Their candy bars also strive to build your vocabulary. "Natural Flavours" (spelled the Canadian way) is translated "Saveurs Naturelles" on the Coffee Crisp bar.

The Wunderbar translates "A peanut butter caramel experience!" to "C'est carachidebile!" When I got home, I used a piece of translator software on this phrase. It came out as: "It is carachidebile!" confirming my suspicion that they had made up a French word as the only way to describe this curious, German-Viking candy bar.

# August

## Time off the dusty trail

I took the month of August off from the hike. I needed some time to let my broiled brain and body recover from the 829 miles I had covered since beginning the adventure in April. And was looking forward to some time to be with my sons and help them move at the beginning of the school year.

Lucas had spent most of the long summer in Shanghai, China. He had been there for 13 weeks, and that separation was getting tough toward the end of that long span. Well, at least for me it had been. We spoke weekly using Skype, and that helped me to know he was doing well. It was nice to actually see him on the computer screen, to see his dorm room, to watch him hold up different foods and drinks he was trying while on the other side of the world. But you can't hug your kid on Skype. He would return mid-month, with just a few weeks before he moved back to Ann Arbor for his second year of college.

Ben had an even bigger move to make in August: he had accepted a fellowship at Carnegie Mellon in Pittsburgh to begin work on a Ph.D. in electrical engineering. So, less than a week after Luc got back from China, we'd all – Me, Luc and Jim – help Ben move to Pittsburgh. It would be a new city for Ben, a new school and program.

I figured all of the moving would help to keep me in shape, lifting boxes and futons, climbing stairs, wrestling heavy things in and out of vehicles and into their new spaces.

Ben and I jammed a borrowed van full of his things and set out for Pittsburgh. Jim and Luc were going to follow the next day with the rest of Ben's things. On our way to Pittsburgh, Ben and I played the license plate game. We happened to pass a car carrier that was loaded with cars from all over, so we got a huge jump on the rare states. When we quickly gained a list of more than 20 states after just a short time on the road, I got excited.

"Call your brother and challenge him and your dad to a license plate contest," I told Ben.

"I'll text him."

"Right. You guys don't talk on that thing anymore," I said, nodding to his fancy phone. "Does Siri get jealous if you talk to people without including her in the conversation?" Ben texted Luc without taking the bait.

He read Luc's reply. "He doesn't want to do it. He says you drive faster than dad, so we have an advantage since we pass more people."

"Trash-talk him! Tell him he's just afraid we're so much better at the game."

Ben looked down at his phone as he texted. "Mom says you're afraid. She's trash-talking you," he mumbled out loud as his thumbs danced over the little keypad.

"You don't tell someone that you're trash-talking them! You just trash-talk them."

It didn't work. Ben's too nice to trash-talk. We drove along happily, continuing the license plate quest. We were playing for our own glory.

We even saw a plate from Rhode Island.

Rhode Island!


When we looped and twirled and up-and-downed our way into Pittsburgh (have you ever driven there? With all those bridges and tunnels and levels?!), the realtor was waiting at the hulking house that had been carved up into apartments for students. She handed Ben the keys and pointed to a door at the bottom of the stairs. Ben had been late in searching for an apartment, so he was lucky to even find a place in the neighborhood he wanted, but his place was in the basement. Technically, it was half in the basement.

Ben jiggled and wiggled the lock on his apartment until the door finally opened. We stepped inside and were hit with a strong mildew smell. Yikes. The next many hours were spent wiping down the place with bleach and shopping for a good air purifier, a filtering vacuum cleaner, and air fresheners. When Jim and Luc arrived the next morning, we had transformed the place from a subterranean dungeon where you might film a horror movie with scratch-and-sniff-and-recoil elements *(the camera pans the room, then zooms in as scary music heightens the tension – what's on the inside of those cupboards?!)* to a fresh-smelling, livable apartment.

We shopped for the things Ben still needed and stocked up on all sorts of lamps and lights for the place. By the end of day two, the apartment was downright pleasant. Ben took us on a tour of campus and showed us the building where he would work and study. It looked to be one of the oldest structures at the university. The entry reached out from the rest of the building with a concave curve scooped out of it to form a sheltered place that you pass through before entering. This entry featured red brick set in a herringbone pattern, trimmed with marble carved to look like leaves framing the wide, double doors. The transom window above the doors was divided into little arcs of glass.

We had a nice time together as a family. Jim and I had been able to work together and put the welfare of our boys first for so long, and I was glad we were still able to do that.

Pittsburgh has a lot going for it. The city has had to reimagine itself after the collapse of the domestic steel industry, and they have done that brilliantly. Andrew Carnegie was a steel magnate – he merged his company with Federal Steel to create U.S. Steel – and he eventually devoted most of his vast fortune to education and philanthropy. The hundreds of Carnegie Libraries scattered across the country are part of this legacy.

Less than two weeks later, Luc and I loaded up the car with his stuff and headed for Ann Arbor. I was worried about what horrors we might find in another "adventure in student housing," but Luc assured me that his apartment was on the second floor, so at least we wouldn't have a subterranean element to deal with. We first drove to my sister's house, as Luc had stored some things there for the summer. Leslie helped us load their truck, then we set off with two vehicles. The day was supposed to get into the mid-90s, not ideal for moving, especially when Luc told us that, no, the apartment didn't have air conditioning.

Lucas's apartment house at the University of Michigan was very near to the central campus, but set back from the road and surrounded by mature trees. Inside, the house was in great shape. Luc headed up the stairs to the second floor and opened the door to his apartment to reveal . . . another set of stairs.

"Oh," he said. "I guess we're on the third floor."

Yes, indeed. Third floor, 94 degrees, let's move all this stuff!

The move went well and no one fainted from the heat. And climbing all those stairs kept my legs toned for the final 176 miles left in my journey.

# September

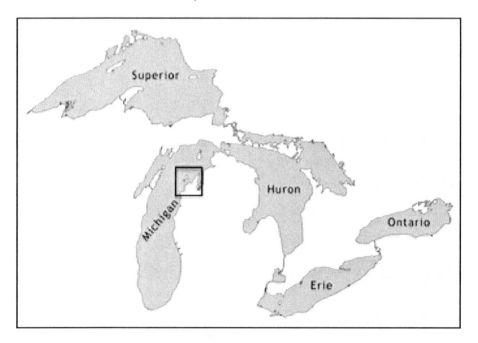

**Suttons Bay to Ludington, Michigan,
Manitou Islands;
Lake Michigan**

**158 miles in 13 days**

## Back to my lake

With both boys off to a good start in the new school year, I headed back to the lakeshore, this time back to Lake Michigan. I had hiked a few miles along this lake after reaching Mackinaw City on my Lake Huron leg of this adventure, but I wanted to continue to explore Lake Michigan's shoreline in September. Those of you who read my first book might be thinking, "Why did she hike Lake Michigan again? She walked all the way around it already! She should have spent more time on the other lakes."

To you I say: *The person doing the 1,000-mile hike gets to make the rules.*

Many people were surprised that I had not made it to the tip of the Leelanau Peninsula on my first adventure. They pointed out the beauty of Michigan's "pinky" that forms the western edge of Grand Traverse Bay. And I agree with them. It's just that I had been running short of time on my first hike; being new to the long-distance hiking thing, some of my planning had been over-ambitious. On that first hike, I had made it to the town of Leland, but then cut across the middle of the peninsula to Suttons Bay on the other side. I had not explored the top half of Michigan's "pinky."

The Leelanau was one of the areas I wanted to explore more fully on this hike, and I wanted to walk the entire length of the shoreline of Sleeping Bear Dunes National Lakeshore, another beautiful, wild stretch. In 2009, I had walked on M-22 part of the way. This time – with the lake level at its lowest ever recorded – I would be able to walk the shoreline the entire way.

I also planned to explore the Manitou Islands a bit. These two islands with a fascinating history of their own lie just off the Sleeping Bear Dunes, and are also part of the National Lakeshore.

So, I drove north to Suttons Bay, a lovely village about halfway up the peninsula, lofted my pack onto my back, and began walking north to the Grand Traverse Lighthouse at the tip of the "pinky."

M-22 winds up the eastern edge of this point of land, heading to the lovely town of Northport. The road is often within sight of the waters of Grand Traverse Bay. The Leelanau Peninsula is prime orchard land, and I passed many groves of fruit trees. Normally the apple trees would be heavy with fruit, but that April had been a brutal month, not at all like the typical mild spring. Instead, the region was struck with multiple hard freezes. With summerlike temperatures in March, all the fruit trees had flowered early, only to have those tender blossoms frozen off in April. Michigan wasn't the only place affected; many of the orchards from the Midwest to the east coast lost the majority of their tree fruit crop. The famous Michigan cherry crop was devastated, and the Traverse City Cherry Festival had to import cherries for the event.

So, as I walked, the orchards were eerily quiet, the storage barns deserted. The weathered, wooden packing crates for apples were stacked neatly outside, empty.

I was hiking to the Grand Traverse Lighthouse, and I found myself mulling over the idea of this day being very "Woolfian" (since Virginia Woolf wrote *To the Lighthouse*). I was pleased with this twining of the literary with my journey and was looking forward to telling Pamela Grath, the owner of Dog Ear Books in Northport, that my day, "Feels very Woolfian . . . as I hike . . . *to the lighthouse."* I would give her a half-smile and wait for her to smile in return (which would take no more than two milliseconds, since Pamela is one of the most voracious readers I know).

Unfortunately, the bookstore was not open when I arrived in Northport. A note on the door said they had survived a busy summer and were taking some well-earned time off. I left her a note stuck in the door. The little joke was still pent up inside me, though, so I told it to my backpack and laughed out loud at the absurdity of it.

One sure thing about lighthouses: they are near the water. The Grand Traverse Lighthouse is a beauty. It graces the top of Michigan's pinky, occupying that tip of land, well buffered by state park around it. I had volunteered as a keeper here a few years back and had kept in touch with the executive director of the nonprofit organization that manages the site, Stef Staley. When I told her I was hiking her way, she told me they'd grill something up for dinner that night.

About two miles from the lighthouse, I passed a self-serve fruit stand on the side of the road. I spotted a few peaches, so I bought some to grill with dinner.

Yes, grilled peaches. Amazing.

The evening proved to be warm and calm, perfect for a cookout and dinner on the lakeshore.

That day ended with one of the most dramatic sunsets I've ever seen on the lake (or anywhere else, for that matter). There were some high cirrus clouds overlaid with some contrails from jets. The contrails had smudged and widened, but not dissipated in the humid, calm day so they formed an abstract crisscross pattern above the horizon. As the sun set, it made the lake and sky glow orange, then fierce red. The contrails and clouds lit up bright golden above the sun's red orb as it descended into the lake. The sun seemed to enlarge as it descended, looking more like a fiery planet than a sun. The clouds striped its surface with red streaks just before it plunged into the lake.

It was a sunset so exotic and brilliant I wanted to pause it, suspend the moment, and sit there for hours basking in it. But, like any sunset, it sped up as it reached perfection. Our closest star slipped into the water, glowed brilliant red, then was slowly extinguished. The sky glowed for a time after the sun had set, slowly tarnishing from gold to bronze.

The next day I hiked the lakeside of the peninsula, heading toward the town of Leland. As I hiked south, I could soon see North Manitou Island. The waterway between the mainland and these islands is called the Manitou Passage. While it appears to be a gentle stretch of water sheltered by the islands, it is actually quite treacherous, as there is only a narrow corridor that is safe for larger boats to move through. There are many ships that have run aground and wrecked in this area. In fact, the lake was so low this year that I saw an old boiler from a shipwrecked steamer exposed in the water about fifty feet offshore. Many more wrecks are scattered, submerged, here and there in the passage or exposed near the islands.

It rained on me most of the day. At one point while I was walking on large flat stones, my boot slipped and I found myself sprawled on the ground, catching myself at the last moment with my hands. I wrestled myself and my pack back up to a sitting position and stayed there a moment as my heartbeat raced. The stones were slick with the rain. I was unhurt, but I could tell that fatigue from hiking in the heat the day before still clung to me.

I moved to the partial shelter of a tree, shrugged off my pack and sat next to it. I looked out at the rain speckling the surface of the lake. Small waves rolled in, and the sky grew darker with leaden rain clouds. I looked at the leaves of the tree and saw a pale, cream-colored spider there. I studied it as I listened to the rain and waves, smelled the lake smells, breathed in the clean air. When I looked out at the lake, I could see the dark outline of North Manitou Island, miles offshore.

Both Manitou Islands are part of the Sleeping Bear Dunes National Lakeshore, and I planned to explore them as part of this adventure. I would spend four days on North Manitou, the more rugged and larger island. The south island had designated campsites, but the north was all backcountry camping. You went out into the wilderness and set up camp where you liked (following guidelines to stay away from water sources).

As the rain continued to fall, I shouldered my pack and headed on, hoping that my days to come on the island would not include rain and slipping and sprawling on rocks.

After checking into my hotel in the town of Leland and dropping my pack in the room, I walked around Fishtown a bit. Leland used to have a thriving fishery. Boats would bring their catch to the river docks there and sell fresh fish from little shanties. There were also smokehouses to preserve some of the catch. In the early 20th century, there were hundreds of fishing tugs harvesting the fish from the lake.

The fishery is mostly gone now, but Leland has preserved this connection to the past. You can walk through historic Fishtown and see some of the fishing vessels docked at the river. The distinctive steel-hulled tug, the *Janice Sue,* is docked there, and one of the shops in Fishtown sells items branded with the silhouette of the distinctive ship. Other shops have filled the old shanties with everything from clothing to shoes to antique glass globes once used to float fishing nets. The Carlson family still fishes the waters of Lake Michigan as they have for over 100 years and you can buy the catch of the day at their store there.

I planned to take a day off in Leland before heading out to North Manitou Island. Since there was such great shopping in the area, Milene and Leslie had decided to meet up with me there during my short break. As a surprise, they picked up Milene's daughter, Alexandra, from Lansing where she is in medical school and brought her along. When they arrived, we had lunch at the Cove Restaurant overlooking the spillway on the river. Leslie ordered a special drink exclusive to Leland, the "Chubby Mary." This is a regular Bloody Mary with a smoked chub fish stuck in it. And it's a whole fish, so it's looking back at you as you sip your drink. Leslie said it gave a smokiness to the drink and the drink gave a spiciness to the fish (which she munched).

These three women are formidable shoppers. We shopped so hard and accumulated so many bags that I was longing to loft my 35-pound pack onto my back. On Sunday, they saw me off at the dock as I boarded the ferry with my pack and my trusty wooden walking stick.

I waved to the three of them as the boat powered out of the marina and into the rolling lake. I waved until I could no longer make out the bright green dot of Leslie's coat, then I turned and faced forward, toward the lake, toward the Manitou Islands.

## Manitou, the Great Spirit

The Native American word "Manitou" has been used to name many places in North America. The Manitou Islands use the name, but there are many other places, including the Canadian Province of Manitoba, the Wisconsin city of Manitowoc, and Ontario's Manitoulin Island (to name a few) that use it for the root of their names. The word, to the native peoples, meant "Great Spirit," and the Manitou Islands were considered to be special and holy places. North Manitou Island has evidence of habitation dating back to 600 B.C.

There is a legend that tells the story of this corner of Michigan: A mother black bear and her two cubs swam across the lake, fleeing a forest fire in Wisconsin. The mother made it to land and rested there, waiting for her cubs, but they were lost in the depths of the lake. The legend says that the Great Spirit Manitou lifted the islands out of the depths where the cubs died. The mother was transformed into the massive Sleeping Bear Dune, always waiting there for her cubs.

Honestly, this story always makes me sad. The legend has been adapted into several lovely children's books that I'm glad I never read as a kid. Drowning cubs? The mom made it and waits on shore forever for her cubs that will never arrive because they drown? I don't care how you spin that story to a kid – *It's okay, honey, the cubs are now ISLANDS and the mom is a SAND DUNE* – I would have been scarred for life, even if I wasn't the most sensitive of kids.

So, as the ferry churned across the choppy twelve miles out to the island, I studied the swirl and froth of the wake from the boat in the cobalt blue water. As we neared the island dock, I looked up to watch the historic village take shape. There were only five of us getting dropped off on North Manitou for the next four days, but there were dozens of people waiting with their backpacks to leave. They had been rained on for the previous two days and looked, as a group, pretty ragged and ready to get back to land and a hot shower.

## Wild wilderness

I expected the island to be wilderness – and most of it is – but as early as the mid-1800s there were people buying up land, logging, and living there.

Logging continued into the early 1900s, and there was a community there that numbered around 200 people for much of this period. The island was also a summer retreat. Some of that history remains to be explored.

The village where the ferry docked has the biggest collection of remaining structures. Some of the buildings are used by the park service to house rangers and their equipment, while others are shuttered and decaying.

I said farewell to the other campers – two retired couples – and set off with my pack on the shoreline heading toward the southern tip of the island. I planned to hike the perimeter of the island in the first two days and wanted to make it to the opposite side of the island before nightfall to set up camp.

I walked the sandy beach with its scattered rocks as waves pulsed at the shoreline. There was quite a bit of algae in the shallows, and it gathered in the curves of the beach. I hiked inland on a short loop at the south end of the island to see the cemetery. The graveyard was a small grassy area, cordoned off with wire fence strung between hand-hewn posts. The names of those buried there are inscribed on a weathered wooden board. The graves themselves were unmarked. I took a break in the woods with a view of the lake and sat underneath a tree to have a snack.

The ferry had departed moments after loading up the campers who were leaving and had already crossed the few miles between the islands by the time I took my break. The ranger who had given us a talk about the island had also left on a smaller boat for Leland. So, it was just five campers and a couple of rangers on an island of over 15,000 acres. There is something about being on a wilderness island that is even more removed from civilization than hiking in a remote place on the mainland.

I looked out at the turquoise watery band near the island; it then merged into the blackest of blues as the bottom of the lake fell off to great depths. I could still see the Leelanau Peninsula at the horizon, a band of cottony clouds hovered above it, but the twelve miles of water separating me from it might as well have been a thousand. This wilderness experience felt even more removed from civilization than my time on Lake Superior with my son Ben, but maybe it was having Ben's company on that stretch that civilized that wild and wondrous stretch of lakeshore.

When I reached the island's southernmost point, I could look across the few miles of water and see the dune bluffs of South Manitou Island. Even this narrow crossing could be treacherous, and souls had been lost here. About halfway between the island and Pyramid Point on the mainland (a perched dune northeast of Glen Arbor), a lighthouse sits atop a concrete crib on a shallow shoal there.

Large flocks of gulls and cormorants and merganser ducks favored the southern end of the island. They took flight and circled around to land behind me (gulls) or fled as a flock out onto the lake (cormorants and ducks) as I approached. I saw many canine tracks on the beach. They were too big for fox, so I suspected they were probably coyote, although the ranger had not mentioned anything about the island having coyote.

As I came around the bottom of the island, large chunks of wooden boats long wrecked here were exposed on the stony shore and in the shallows. There is such beauty in wood that has been weathered and worn by waves and the elements for many decades. The craftsmanship of these vessels is still evident, even as time has worn away and bent the metal pegs holding the structure together.

I passed many bird carcasses and the picked-clean skeletons of fish and deer on the shore. A Great Blue Heron fished in the shallows studded with boulders. The sunlight glittered on the water as the sun lowered in the sky and a dune arose along the shoreline, cutting me off from the interior of the island.

I wanted to reach the site where the logging city of Crescent once thrived. I knew that the only intact structure there is a huge barn, and I wanted to see it before I set up camp nearby. I hustled to a gap in the dunes where the city had been located – the pilings from the city's pier still remain in the lake there – and I hiked up a trail toward the barn. At the highest point of the trail there was a clearing in the woods that people had used as a campsite. Off the clearing, there were several trails, which seemed to branch and curl around aimlessly with no markings to show which one led to the barn. The land was rolling and wooded, so the barn could have been nearby and I would not have seen it.

In fact, it was and I didn't. I set off on a more direct heading toward the trail marked on my GPS since I was losing light and wanted to see the barn, set up camp, and eat dinner before I was pitched into complete darkness. The moon wouldn't rise until after midnight.

This more direct route took me through a mostly dry bog, but the hiking was still difficult due to the characteristic hillocks and low semi-mucky terrain there. I scared up a large deer from the bog and watched it high-hurdle its way gracefully out of sight. After thrashing through the tall grasses and mucky places and over several rolling hills, I reached the main trail and decided to head to the north. Wrong choice for the barn it turned out, but a sign marked the side trail leading to the former site of the settlement of Crescent. I took that back toward the lake and looked for a good place to set up my hammock tent, obeying the rule of staying 300 feet away from the lake. I found a place in a stand of cedar trees and put down my backpack. Then, I looked at the plants all around me: poison ivy.

I had even set my pack down on poison ivy.

I wasn't sure I had ever seen so much poison ivy growing in one area before. Shouldering my pack, I backed away, fervently hoping I wouldn't be regretting this encounter for the next week or two.

I found a couple of trees in a small valley between two wooded dunes and strung my hammock and boiled water for my dinner. The valley gave me a small view of the water, but the sun did not cooperate and set at that exact spot.

I had hiked most of the day and was still recovering from the previous day's shopping excursion in Leland, so not long after sunset I climbed into my hammock tent and into my sleeping bag and fell asleep in an instant.

A spotlight awoke me after midnight. It was so bright I thought it was a flashlight someone was holding against the mesh of my tent, but it was just the moon. It had crept up and over the dune and shone so brightly that it startled me out of my sleep. I took a moment to get out, stretch, and look at the moon and thousands of stars. The night was chilly, so I jumped around a bit, appreciating the clarity of the night, the sharpness of detail in the moonlight, then climbed back into my swinging shelter, curled in a ball, and fell back to sleep.

## Sand sculptures and the Swenson barn

The next day I stowed my camping gear and shouldered my pack and continued hiking north, determined to circle the island in two days. Not far from camp, I came across the markings of a struggle in the sand. A very large winged creature had been pounced on by a coyote, and from the bloody splotches in the sand, it had lost the battle. Its wingtips had pressed into the sand many times, leaving beautiful stroke marks. This grand bird had struggled and thrashed mightily before giving up its life to nourish the lives of the coyotes.

I found a footprint of the bird: a Great Blue Heron.

Not too far from this tableau, I noticed that the large coyote prints were interspersed with smaller ones: pups.

On the northwest side of the island, the sand gives way to a cobble-stone-strewn shoreline with tall, wooded dunes narrowing the corridor I walked. The Manitous are part of a chain of islands in northeastern Lake Michigan that were formed by glacial till, debris dropped by retreating gla-ciers that piled up on the edge of a limestone shelf underneath the water here. As I looked up at the dunes that were hundreds of feet above the lake level, I marveled at the amount of sand and rock carried by the glaciers.

Those ancient ice sheets would have dwarfed these soaring dunes, though, because the ice was at least a mile tall. I contemplated the amount of material deposited into the lakes and on the land by these continental ice walls that scoured the area for so many years, dredging out the lakebeds, scrubbing the land, then redistributing glacial till as they retreated.

Ancient glacial moraines on the land and even on the floor of the lakes mark the paths of the advance and retreat of successive glaciers. The force exerted by these mountains of ice is difficult to imagine, but the way they marked and shaped the land is still evident today.

On North Manitou Island, the exposed face of the dunes reveals the striations and sorting of the glacial till, with alternating sand and rock layers banding the dunes. There are places where these perched dunes had sloughed off, sliding sand and rock into the lake. Several trees had tumbled down with one slide; they were uprooted and tangled, half stuck in the water. Groundwater seeped from the face of the dune. In one area, it had gathered the coarse sand and formed drip sculptures, like kids make with a bucket of wet sand on the beach.

I set up camp near the village, planning to sleep there for the next two nights. The following day I was able to hike the interior loop of trail carry-ing only my water bottle and walking stick, giving my backpack a day off from the hike.

There are signposts on the trails as you hike out of the village carved with the words: Entering Wilderness. Along the path, though, there are reminders of the people who once lived there: an old homestead, a junked truck, an old apple tree, or rose bushes so ancient their canes were thicker than my thumb.

I encountered these ancient rose bushes at my camp near Crescent City. By "encounter," I mean I walked right into one at dusk and had to extricate myself from its grasp. The bush radiated from a central point, but then the canes arced out and looped about the area, untended for decades. While hiking the interior of the island the following day, I discovered a splinter in the knuckle of my middle finger. When I finally worked it out, I discovered it was a thick thorn from that rose bush.

On the main trail, I met up with one of the couples that had been dropped with me on the island, and they directed me to the barn that I had missed the day before. The Swenson Barn is long and low, its metal roof streaked with rust, its wooden sideboards mostly denuded of the red paint that once made it stand out against the landscape. It looked like it was fading into nature, as tree branches reached to embrace it and scrub grew up along its flanks.

I have a thing for barns and found this one to be beautiful. I walked through the open door and saw fishing nets bundled on the dirt floor. There were many footprints from hikers and even an area where some numbskull had tried to make a fire *inside the barn.* I gasped and walked on to examine the rest of the place. There were stanchions for cows, and a room with stacks of old wooden windows with multiple small panes leaning against the walls. Most of the glass panes were broken; the intact ones were caked with dust.

As I left the barn and hiked through the woods to the lake, I had a feeling that I was being watched. I turned my head and was greeted by the outstretched arms of a praying mantis, perched on my shoulder. I tilted my head to get a better look at him, and he tilted his triangle head back at me. He seemed pretty happy to have hitched a ride, but I figured he'd have better luck hunting from a stationary perch, so I lifted him and let him walk off my hand onto the smooth bark of a beech tree.

The wind picked up more each day I was on the island, and at times at night my hammock tent was transformed into a trampoline. The constant breeze gave a gentle sway to the trees and my sleeping structure, which was mostly pleasant, like being rocked to sleep. But when an extra-strong gust blasted through, the trees thrashed and bucked, and my hammock tossed me up and down. Exciting!

On the third day on the island, I met up with a ranger and got a chance to ask him about the coyotes.

"Yes, they've been on the island five years now," he said. "Both islands. Probably came over on the ice."

"I saw pup tracks near the northwest corner of the island," I told him.

He nodded. "I hear them yipping at night sometimes."

The day was windy, and the trees overhead kept whipping around. Out on the lake, the water was choppy with whitecaps.

"Do you think the ferry will come if the lake is rough like this?" I asked.

"Probably not. I'll find out when I call in the morning," he said.

Now this was unfortunate. I had brought a bit of extra food in case the ferry was delayed, but my rule when hiking is to eat my favorite things first, so the extra stuff was not my favorite. I could try to save some of my mac & cheese by not eating it all that night, but that idea kind of made me sad. And my chocolate was almost gone.

And what if I was marooned on North Manitou for longer than a single extra day?

Tragedy loomed.

The next day I checked in with the ranger. He said the ferry was going to make the run to the island, even though the high winds hadn't calmed down and the lake still looked rough.

I broke camp and packed my backpack up with everything – including part of the mac & cheese I had bravely denied myself the night before – and hiked to the village. I was a little disappointed with the thought of leaving this wonderful island. Other than the gusty winds, the weather had been perfect these four days: no rain, warm nights.

The two couples and I converged at a picnic table by the dock, and the ranger stopped by to tell us that the ferry would stop only briefly since the lake was so rough. When we saw it approaching, we should hustle onto the dock and get ready to board.

When the time came, we dashed out and sprang onto the rocking vessel. Most of the people on the ferry looked a little queasy; several lost their breakfast in the next section of the loop as we crossed the rough water between the two islands to dock at South Manitou. The dock there was more sheltered, and the ferry remained there for several hours, as most of the people took a guided tour of the island. I hung out with the other campers near the ranger's station for a bit, then we scattered to explore on our own. I hiked onto the beach, then doubled back toward the lighthouse. South Manitou has a natural harbor that is deep enough for even the largest of ships to take refuge there during storms. This island is only a third as big as North Manitou, but gets more visitors who want to do the guided tour on a day trip, as well as more campers wanting a more organized experience.

On my short walk to the lighthouse, by my calculations I reached a milestone: 900 miles hiked on this adventure. I took this moment to reflect on these wild islands named by the Native Americans after their Great Spirit, and on the surrounding waters of the Great Lakes. It is astonishing to consider how modern man has tamed and contorted and even changed the flow of these waters at times (the flow of the Chicago River was altered to flow away from Lake Michigan instead of into it over a century ago). How we've introduced species from the other side of the planet into these inland seas, industrialized their connecting rivers, and drained and destroyed vast, cleansing wetlands.

This milestone of my hike took place on an island that remains relatively wild, forever protected. The Manitou Islands are to be enjoyed, but never lumbered or farmed again. These islands were once holy to the native tribes, and now modern man has also revered them by cloaking them with the protection of the National Lakeshore designation. As I walked to the sentinel light along the rock-strewn beach, I studied the beautiful rocks and watched a cormorant plunge repeatedly underneath incoming waves, until I finally arrived at the light in a white tower on the rugged island shore.

As we made our way back to Leland, I studied the water from the top of the ferry. The winds on the lake had calmed a bit, but the black water still roiled with energy, wavy and rippled, like fractured obsidian made to flow.

In Leland I loaded my backpack up front in the passenger seat of my car and we made a stop at the grocery store. I was happy to buy fresh provisions: apples and a sandwich with tomatoes and a smoothie made of fruit and veggies – a great antidote to freeze-dried food. And I stocked up on chocolate again.

## Frogabunga?

The Sleeping Bear Dunes National Lakeshore stretches from west of Leland on Good Harbor Bay almost all the way to the Point Betsie Lighthouse north of Frankfort. On my first hike, I had walked much of this impressive shoreline, but not all of it. Part of the time I walked on M-22.

This time, I would be able to walk every step at the water's edge. The reason was that the lake was even lower than it was in 2009. I knew that this time there should be a corridor that would allow me to walk around places that were reported to be underwater a few years ago.

If any of you who read the first book are still wondering why I would retrace any steps from my first journey, I have to tell you that this National Lakeshore is my favorite stretch of Great Lakes shoreline. I'm not alone in this opinion. This area was voted the most beautiful place in America by ABC's *Good Morning America* in 2011, and the number of visitors to the park in 2012 had just set a new record, managing to break the all-time high the week my pack and I were hiking there.

I liked to think that maybe my visit was the one to break the old record.

The park contains a series of three bays: Good Harbor Bay, Sleeping Bear Bay, and the most southern – and largest – Platte Bay. These gentle arcs of shoreline are punctuated with two massive perched dunes at the two points separating the three bays. The first point is called Pyramid Point. The second is Sleeping Bear Point. Other dunes fill in the gaps between these giants, and the park reaches inland to protect the ecology of the dunes and their surrounding terrain, so the park encompasses over 100 square miles.

Oh, they are gorgeous dunes and bays! And some lovely towns break up the parkland: Glen Arbor and Empire are two lovely cities along the shoreline, while Frankfort and Leland are at either end. My plan was to hike the entire shoreline – over 35 miles from Leland to Frankfort – in three days.

The first day I was elated to be on this magnificent shoreline again. Even though it was overcast and occasionally sprinkled on me, that happiness never dissipated. I came upon a group of seven turkey vultures hanging out on the shore, perched on a large log and walking around in the sand. I knew there had been an increasing number of these large, scavenging birds, but had never seen this large a grouping on the beach. Studies show that their population has steadily increased in the Great Lakes region for the past fifty years.

The vultures mainly eat road kill, so more roads built over the years has meant more dinner for them. More recently, cuts in municipal budgets were also having an effect; I walked through a number of communities in Michigan where I learned they had stopped picking up road kill as a way to save money for other city services. In those places, it was like a nonstop buffet for scavengers. And the lakeshore also provides take-out for these birds as large fish and dead birds wash up on the beach.

As I got near to the log, I could see that there was, in fact, a meal on the sand there. The vultures reluctantly flew off as I approached to identify what it was: a cormorant, picked bloody by the scavengers.

A scurrying group of sanderlings ran along the water's edge farther up the beach. These birds are the hardest workers amongst shorebirds, constantly examining what each wave deposits on the packed sand. Beetles and butterflies, ducks and gulls, sandpipers and frogs also lived at this edge where water meets land.

I had started to feel at home on this edge, too.

I startled one frog, and she jumped into the waves and body-surfed along, tumbling at first, then righting herself with her strong back legs. She took more one tumble as a big curling wave swept in, and I yelled, "Cowabunga!"

I didn't know if there was a frog equivalent.

"*Frogabunga?*"


## Salmon-a-spawning

When I made it around the western edge of Good Harbor and entered Sleeping Bear Bay, I could again see both Manitou Islands. I hiked around Pyramid Point, under the 400-foot perched dune that has held its place here since the retreat of the last glacier. There were places where there was just a narrow band of rocks to walk between the foot of the dune and the water, but it was passable all the way to Crystal River.

Spring had come early this year, and the timing of the salmon had been thrown off a bit. While they usually spawn in October, they were making their way up the Crystal River a couple of weeks early, making the pilgrimage this year in September. All of the salmon found in the Great Lakes populations today have been planted there by the Department of Natural Resources. Chinook and Coho are native to the Pacific Ocean. These fish are stocked in the lakes to support the sport-fishing industry, and each fall they follow their wild compulsion to move up the waterways that feed into the lakes and spawn.

I walked along the riverbank, watching the salmon gather to rest before heading upstream. The water in the river was low, and half of the mouth was obstructed with sand. These salmon are beautiful fish. Each is well over a foot and a half long, sleek and muscular from living in the rough waters of the lake, from chasing quick shiny alewives for dinner. As I watched a large group of them start to swim up the narrow river, I noticed one fish that looked different from the rest. It had a huge lamprey attached to its side just behind the gill. I had never seen one of these out in the lakes, let alone attached to a fish. The lamprey was almost as long as the salmon, and the salmon did not look happy to have this parasite sucking away at its life.

Well, the salmon looked as unhappy as a salmon can look. They rarely look happy, even on a good day, even when everything is going their way.

Each lamprey will consume around forty pounds of fish in their lifetime. I wondered if this salmon would be able to spawn, to propagate its species before succumbing to the vampire fish suctioned onto its side.

The three days hiking this shoreline from Leland to the Point Betsie Lighthouse were wonderful, mostly solitary days. People only congregated at the two rivers where the salmon gathered. The salmon carried the hopes of the next generation of their kind; the people carried rods and reels, flies and creels, hoping to advance their own salmon dreams.

As I approached the foot of the Pierce Stocking Overlook, a place where it is possible to climb down the 450-foot dune to the lake, I wondered what the two dark motionless dots were on the middle of the dune. I realized they were people who were sitting there taking a break from their climb up the mountain of sand. I waved to them, and they waved back.

The flock of turkey vultures caught the thermals off of the dune and circled constantly overhead without exerting any effort. The dead carcasses of ducks and cormorants dotted the shoreline, many half-consumed by the soaring cleanup crew. They waited for me to pass before returning to their job.

During part of my hike, I had seen a good amount of algae on the lake. Its increase correlates with the increase in the invasive mussel population. This aquatic plant needs a surface to grow on, so as mussels populate and spread on the bottom of the lakes, the algae has more places to attach itself to. While you might envision this as some fuzzy patches of green algae here and there underneath the water, the situation is more dramatic. When storms rile the lakes, algae is often stripped from where it is growing, and it floats to the surface. There is now so much algae in the lake that scientists use satellite images to view floating rafts of algae. After one summer storm in 2010, they estimated that 6,000 tons of the green stuff had been dislodged, just in the area around the Manitou Islands.

Some scientists, including Dr. Stephen Riley at the Great Lakes Research Center, believe that decaying algae can create dead zones when it settles again on the lakebed; these areas become deprived of oxygen. In these pockets, anaerobic bacteria like *clostridium botulinum* (which is found naturally in the environment) can thrive. Under certain conditions this bacteria produces a potent paralyzing toxin, the very same substance that is marketed under the name "botox" to paralyze facial muscles so people don't get wrinkles. In the lake, these toxins are concentrated in the zebra and quaga mussels (which constantly filter the water) and then the poisons accumulate in the creatures that feed on the mussels, including the round goby fish. When the goby fish become paralyzed and float to the surface, birds eat them. When the birds take in the toxin, they become sluggish and uncoordinated. If they take in too much, they are paralyzed too; they lose their ability to breathe, and die.

This botulism/dead-bird connection has proven to be increasingly lethal as the lake levels fall and as the lake temperature increases. During my hike, Lake Michigan was receding to a level lower than ever recorded since scientists have been taking measurements of the lakes, a new historic low. And the warm summer had heated the lakes to new highs.

And dead birds were stacking up on the lakeshore, attracting flocks of circling turkey vultures.

Since I had my car along on this leg of my hike (friends would shuttle my car for me, or B&B owners would drive me back to pick up my car after I had hiked all day), I decided to stop and do the Empire Bluffs Trail south of the city of Empire. If you've ever seen the "Pure Michigan" ad, with its magnificent, sweeping view up the shoreline where wooded dunes give way to a sandy perched dune, it was shot from this trail.

There are quite a few steps to get from the lakeshore up to that vantage point, but it is not a very long trail, and the steps are gentle. I've been up this way several times, but never tire of the view from the top. Today, it was a great vantage point to survey around twenty miles of what I had already walked. I could also marvel at the crescent of land-meets-water that is Platte Bay. I could see the Sleeping Bear Dune, the sad mythical mother still awaiting the return of her island cubs. Or I could sit and just look down at the waves caressing the sandy shore below.

I hiked from Frankfort south to Arcadia in one day, a day that threatened to storm, but never delivered. The sky was dramatic and close as I hiked the deserted shore with only my pack for company. The lake turned from blue to green to black as the sky darkened, and the water frothed from being whipped by the winds.

## Lumbering and a heroine of the sky

When I reached the town of Arcadia, Patrice, the owner of the Arcadia House B&B, announced she had arranged for me to have a personal tour of the historical museum in town.

"I called Joyce," she said. "She'll open the museum for you at 9:30 tomorrow morning, so you can see it before you leave."

"Just for me?"

"She's happy to do it."

Joyce is the great granddaughter of Samuel Gilbert, the man who founded the town of Arcadia. One of the rooms in the museum was devoted to the founder's family, and Joyce pointed out her relatives in the photos, "My cousin, my great uncle . . ." she pointed to the sepia faces staring back at us. Joyce was only around five foot tall, but she took charge like a much taller person. She had very little gray in her hair even though she was several years retired from teaching, and when I looked at her toes peaking out of her open-toed wedges, I noticed that her toenails were polished to match her outfit, a demure taupe.

We walked into the main room and Joyce pointed to a photo of Arcadia Lake at the height of the lumbering era. The lake was clogged with floating logs, mills ringed the water, and cut lumber was stacked neatly on docks in the foreground. Joyce pointed out various structures, then said, "I wish I could have lived in that time."

I was surprised, considering the painted toenails.

"This was more than a lumber town," Joyce said. "There was a mirror factory and a furniture factory." In a side room of the museum she showed me antique mirrors. An explanation told how to make a silver-backed mirror by mixing silver nitrate with ammonia to precipitate a silver film onto a glass plate. I had seen old mirrors where the reflective surface has blackened or flaked over time, but I had never thought about the process of "silvering a mirror" before.

"The biggest business here for years was the furniture factory," Joyce said. She led me to thick ledgers from the factory, massive books with lined, aged paper covered with neat handwriting by an extinct worker assigned to keep track of furniture production. There were pieces of furniture from the factory office and samples of their products. The second story of the museum had rooms filled with dressers, beds, desks, and vanities crafted from trees harvested nearby and shaped into furniture in Arcadia.

"The factory burned twice," she told me. "Once in 1917 when it was a furniture factory. Then again about fifty years later when it was used to house turkeys."

"Turkeys?"

"Turkeys. The whole town smelled like burned feathers after that fire."

She paused for a moment before the door of one of the rooms upstairs. "Have you heard of Harriet Quimby?"

I had not.

"Most people haven't, but she was the first licensed female pilot in America and the first woman to fly over the English Channel."

I was surprised I had not heard of her.

A mannequin sat in the corner of the Harriet Quimby room, a skinny figure with her legs crossed and her hands set atop her knees. She wore the oddest outfit: a purple silk jumpsuit with a pointy hood. Large goggles fit over her eyes. "That's a re-creation of the flying suit she wore," Joyce said, when she saw me staring at the figure.

"Do you want to know *why* you've never heard of her?" she continued. "Because she flew over the English Channel the same day the *Titanic* sank. Her news couldn't compete with that. Then she died shortly after."

As the mannequin's goggled eyes seemed to follow me around the room, I took photos of the articles on display.

"Harriet Quimby was born here in Arcadia, though she never wanted to be known as a farmer's daughter. In fact, she told everyone she grew up in California. We've worked hard to get her accomplishments recognized."

The planes that Harriet Quimby flew were wings and engines stuck onto frames, a mere suggestion of a plane. I couldn't imagine flying something like that over land, let alone over open water. Later reading a book about Quimby, I was surprised to learn that the engines constantly leaked and sprayed oil, so the pilot would have an oil facial by the time she landed.

The book also told about her death in an accident over Boston. Horribly, she and her passenger were tossed out of the plane and fell to their deaths. The author of the book suggested that it was her passenger who may have caused the plane to go into a dive and that Quimby may have unbuckled her safety harness to try to help him.

She got her pilot's license in August of 1911, flew the English Channel in April 1912, and died less than three months later. She was a journalist, an adventurer, a pioneer of flight. Amelia Earhart credited Quimby with inspiring her to take to the skies.

I thanked Joyce for the tour, then drove south to Manistee, a small town on the lake about twenty miles south of Arcadia.

Over the final three days of hiking on Lake Michigan, I covered much of the shoreline between Arcadia and Ludington, first by doing looping hikes from the in between city of Manistee, then a long day hike in Ludington.

The first of these days was windy and cold. The lake was alive with waves crashing on the beach. Whitecaps rolled over the entire surface of the gray-green water. Rain fell from gray-banded clouds out over the lake. Toward the end of the day, hail pelted me as I walked. The day was sharp and present, the weather from the west impossible to ignore.

The next day was calmer and warmer. I saw a pair of bald eagles fly over the lake. They connected, grasping talons, then fell, twirling toward the lake, briefly, before regaining winged flight. I had seen many bald eagles over the lake, but never before their dance in midair.

Near the breakwall by the outflow of the Manistee River, I saw a cormorant sitting on the sand near some rocks. As I approached, I was surprised when it didn't hurry into the water to put some distance between us. Cormorants, in my experience, are skittish. This one watched me approach, then merely tucked its beak underneath its wing. I got within a few feet of the bird and it did not make any effort to move, so I knew it was not well.

## Part of me

I wanted to prolong my time on Lake Michigan, but the miles were stacking up and I almost had enough under my belt, over 980 total miles walked so far, so I knew it was time to contemplate the finale: a hike along the

Niagara River to the great falls. The final leg would allow me to reach my 1,000-mile total in celebratory style, with family and friends and followers at my side.

I planned to finish my Lake Michigan hike in Ludington. On the advice of my friend, Cindy, I head to the Skyline Trail in the state park there. This short, looping trail begins with a steep stair climb. I hustle up the wooden steps. When I reach the top, I have to gasp at the view.

When I look south to the Ludington Harbor Lighthouse, I realize that the day is so clear that I can make out the dunes at Silver Lake about twenty miles past the lighthouse. I crave these vistas and drink them in, consume them, make the sand and waves part of me.

And it is part of me; after hiking almost 2,000 miles (both adventures combined) on the shores of the Great Lakes, drinking their waters, wading and swimming in them, strolling their beaches and bluffs and dunes and paths, attuning all of my senses to these vast inland seas, aren't they part of me, and I a part of them?

I hiked through the woods to get out to the lakeshore. The next few miles will be hiked on that edge where water meets sand. The scent of evergreens wafts on the breeze, and I pluck a few needles from trees as I walk – spruce and pine and fir – and rub them between my fingers to release the scented oils. It is the smell of winter, of pending snowfall that will come soon enough, and Christmas after that.

I cross over the dam and follow the river to where it merges with the lake. The monotone rush of water over the dam fades behind me and is supplanted by the sound of the waves and wind on the lake. This is a more layered and nuanced water sound; an undertone of far-off, rolling water punctuated by waves flopping onto the sand nearby.

I hiked up the shoreline to the Big Sable Lighthouse, a metal-clad, lakeshore marker painted with broad bands of white and black. I circled the sentinel.

And then I headed back the way I came, relishing every remaining step in the soft sand. Before I went inland to return to my car, I took a moment to say farewell to Lake Michigan. While looking out at the waves rolling in, I loosened the shoulder straps of my pack and realized that these are the final moments with my big pack, that I won't need it at the finale. I didn't even need it on my back for this day loop hike, but I emptied most of the gear out of it and strapped it on anyway. I felt incomplete without it since it had been on my back for so many weeks, so many miles. It had been my companion, the ever-present weight on my back, both pushing me down and making me stronger with each step I took.

I wanted to say "We did it" or "Thanks," but that seemed silly to say to the deflated pack on my back, so I just patted the shoulder straps with affection.

Somehow that didn't seem silly at all.

Turning inland, I set my mind on the final miles ahead at the great falling waters of Niagara.

# October

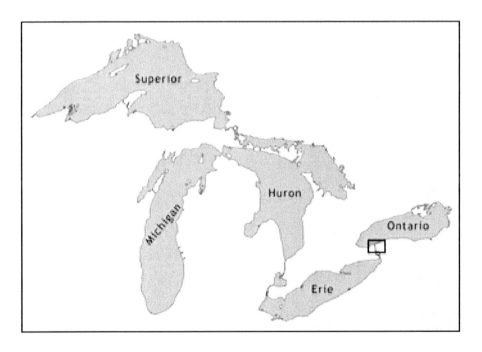

Niagara-on-the-Lake to Niagara Falls, Ontario;
Lake Ontario to Niagara River to Niagara Falls

**18 miles in 2 days**

## "Slowly I turned . . ."

There's an old vaudeville routine that Abbott & Costello and the Three
Stooges did, and I can't think of Niagara Falls without it springing to mind.
The routine hinges on the past of one of the characters. This man tracked
the guy that stole his wife all over the world, and finally catches up with
him at Niagara Falls. The man is so obsessed with this event that anytime
someone mentions the words "Niagara Falls," he is transported back to the
moment he passed this man on the street and turned to confront him.

"Niagara Falls! Slowly I turned, then step-by-step, inch-by-inch, I walked up to him, and I punched him and ripped his shirt and knocked him down!"

The character, fully engrossed in his memories, pummels whatever poor person happened to mention Niagara Falls. It is just the first of several beatings delivered during the skit (every time Niagara Falls was mentioned) to increase the hilarity of the situation.

It's a silly sketch with broad physical comedy, but it always makes me laugh.

This is not the reason I chose Niagara Falls *(slowly I turned . . .)* for the finale of my hike.

I chose the falls because it is the most dramatic place to see the volume of water moving through the Great Lakes system. You see, all of this fresh water is moving to the ocean – slowly, relentlessly. When you stand on the shores of one of these lakes, it seems as if the water is contained there, but it is not so. These waters are connected and they are moving, and their destination is the North Atlantic Ocean.

The mean length of time that water spends in each lake (called the "retention time") is a function of the volume of water each lake holds and how fast the lake is draining into the adjoining body of water. Lake Superior is the largest lake and it drains into Lake Huron via the St. Mary's River. The mean time that water spends in Superior is 191 years.

Lake Michigan's retention time is 99 years.

Lake Huron's: only 22 years.

Erie's is around 3 years, and Ontario's 6 years.

The water from Lake Ontario drains at its northeastern corner into the St. Lawrence River. The water then travels for almost 750 miles – passing by the metropolises of Montreal and Quebec City – before flowing into the Gulf of St. Lawrence, lapping at the shores of Newfoundland and Nova Scotia, and finally merging with the North Atlantic Ocean.

The lakes are connected. And they all flow to the Atlantic.

Superior (via St. Mary's River) and Michigan (via the Straits of Mackinac) both flow into Huron. In turn, Huron drains (via the St. Clair River-Lake St. Clair-Detroit River connection) into Erie. Erie then pushes water north into Ontario (via the Niagara River where the falls are).

Last but not at all least, Ontario drains via the St. Lawrence River to the Atlantic.

Check out the flow on this map:

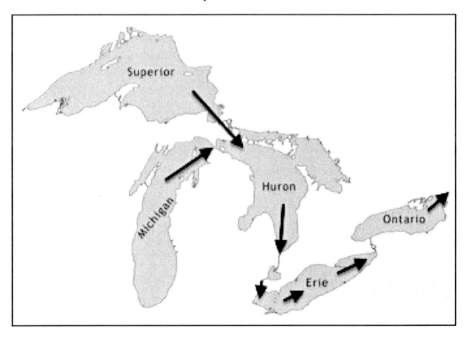

Why does the water move at different speeds from lake to lake? The simple answer is gravity – and the matter of the difference in elevation between the connected lakes. The surface of Lake Superior's water is at 600 feet above sea level, while Huron is at 577 feet, so the water empties briskly south into Lake Huron.

In contrast, Erie is only a few feet lower than Huron, hence the sluggish movement of water between these two lakes.

The most dramatic change in elevation of the lakes, of course, takes place between Erie and Ontario; the surface of Lake Erie is over 300 feet higher than the surface of Lake Ontario. The water descends as it rushes downstream (northward, by compass direction) along the Niagara River, and hits the big drop over Niagara Falls *(slowly I turned . . .)*.

## Walk with me

I invited family and friends and followers to join me in the city of Niagara Falls, Ontario. Together, we would hike the final two days (or just the final two steps, if that was all someone wanted to tackle!) of this adventure. Together, we would witness the dramatic movement of water through the largest freshwater system on the planet. Together, we would hike from the shores of Lake Ontario to the falls and celebrate the completion of this journey.

The Canadian side of the river has a wonderful paved path running along the river from Lake Ontario, past the falls, and south to the shores of Lake Erie. This designated pedestrian and bike pathway is called the Niagara Recreational Trail. This was another reason to conclude my hike here: the pathway allowed me to hike safely with a large group.

We began the upstream hike in the city of Niagara-on-the-Lake, a Canadian town situated at the mouth of the Niagara River where the river calmly merges with Lake Ontario. The waters carry no indication that just a fifteen miles upstream they had hurtled over a massive falls, followed by long stretches of wild rapids.

Two historic forts sit near the mouth of the river. Fort Niagara holds the position on the American side, and Fort George on the Canadian. With such longstanding peace between Canada and the U.S., it's difficult to imagine hostilities across this placid part of the river, but these fortifications, again, tell the tale of The War of 1812.

As I had on other occasions on this long hike, we would be walking where the blood of British and Loyalists and Native Americans and Americans had been spilled and soaked into the ground beneath our feet.

Niagara-on-the-Lake is often described as the prettiest town in Ontario. It is home to a summer festival celebrating the plays of George Bernard Shaw, and the village is full of 19th-century buildings, now hosting inns, restaurants, and shops. Many, many shops.

Leslie and Milene were part of the group that hiked this first day with me. When they saw all the stores in the quaint city of Niagara-on-the-Lake, I thought they would defect to do some shopping. They stuck with the group, though, with only an occasional longing glance back over their shoulders.

This first morning was cool and clear, and the leaves were mostly still on the trees and in full fall color. It was breathtakingly beautiful. The group hiking with me ranged in age from their early twenties to well into their retirement years. I was pleased to see how the group formed, mixed and mingled, and re-formed as we walked, and everyone got acquainted with each other. One of the couples, Mickey and Lynn, had met up with me on the very first day of my hike, months ago in Port Clinton, Ohio, and they wanted to be with me for the last days in Niagara. For me, it was a completely different experience to be surrounded by people instead of the solitary hike I had experienced for the vast majority of my journey. It was also delightful; I mingled with the group and chatted with everyone, enjoying the day and the excellent company.

This first day was an eight-mile hike. That distance, in itself, is a bit of a challenge for a person in average health to walk. The added element was the elevation change. Most of the 300-foot difference in sea level between Lakes Erie and Ontario would be climbed this day as we walked up the Niagara Escarpment, which we would encounter at a place called Queenston Heights. In short, we would reach a long, insistent incline near the end of the first day's walk.

## The Niagara Escarpment and Alfred, the horse

An *escarpment* is a cliff that separates two relatively level areas. It can be formed two ways: either by action along a fault in the earth's crust, a stress line where one plate pushes up another (like in the Rift Valley in Kenya), or through the force of erosion. Unequal erosive forces were the method that formed the Niagara Escarpment: the cap of hard dolomitic limestone ("dolostone") atop the falls is incredibly resistant to erosion. Where this cap exists, the land is much higher than the adjacent areas, where the glaciers and the force of water had easily worn softer shale and other rock and sediments away over time.

The waters of the Niagara River plunge over this escarpment at the falls. If you look into the bend of water as it begins its plunge, you can see the lip of the hard limestone poking off the top of the ledge, giving shape to the water as it curves and cascades.

I had cautioned the group walking with me about the incline that we'd hit at the end of the first day's hike. I hoped I wouldn't have to carry anyone out on my back. Though, after carrying my heavy pack for hundreds of miles, I was certainly in good enough shape to do so if needed.

Two centuries prior to the day we hiked here – almost to the day – shortly after Major-General Isaac Brock and Chief Tecumseh had overrun the American fort at Detroit, Brock had to hurry to Fort George in response to reports that the Americans planned to invade across the Niagara River.

When the Americans crossed near the village of Queenston, Brock rode his horse, Alfred, at a full gallop the seven miles from Fort George to Queenston, tethered Alfred to a tree, and led his men in a charge to attack the Americans.

I've often wondered if the fighting British soldier had any regrets about wearing a red uniform that stood out so well against the colors of nature. At least the Americans chose the more muted blue to blend in a bit. Brock took a musket ball in the wrist during the battle, but still continued in the charge to meet the onslaught of the Americans.

Brock already carried the scars of war. His left eye was permanently closed and he walked with a limp from wounds sustained in the Napoleonic War. There was also a scar on his neck where he had been grazed by a musket ball. He was a tall man, 6'2", and large at around 250 pounds. But he was not invincible; even a man of that stature and fortitude cannot withstand a musket ball to the heart. When he was struck again in this battle, not far from Niagara Falls, he fell and bled to death on the land he was defending. Nonetheless, his men fought on and won the Battle of Queenston.

When Tecumseh heard of Brock's death, he mourned the loss of a great leader and friend. Sadly, Tecumseh would soon fall in battle as Brock had. A musket ball had his name on it; it was also destined for his heart.

There is a little art museum along the Niagara River, and they had mounted a display to commemorate the 200th anniversary of the war. It included the only known portrait that Brock had sat for. It is a small pastel drawing, showing him in profile, revealing his right side only – his left eye may have already been closed. He wears the red uniform of the British soldier, his shoulders festooned with gold epaulets, a white cravat around his scarred throat.

We hiked to the marker on the spot where Alfred had been tethered to wait for the return of his general. There is a small statue of the horse there atop a pedestal, encased in glass: Alfred still saddled and bridled, forever waiting, forever alert, in bronze. Nearby, just a few feet away, is a worn and weathered marker on the spot where Brock was mortally wounded and fell.

We paused by these markers and tried to imagine the hellfire unleashed there two hundred years ago.

We finished the climb to the high point at Queenston where Brock is buried underneath a tall marble column. The monolith is topped with a statue of his likeness, his arm outstretched, leading his troops onward.

From the heights, we could look back on the miles we had walked that day from the shores of Lake Ontario and the city of Niagara-on-the-Lake. The Niagara River nearby was broad and calm as it curved on its way to merge with the final Great Lake in this complex system of vast inland seas. The colorful leaves on the trees on either side of the riverbank looked especially festive against the deep blue of the river.

We hiked the final bit of the trail that day to the Floral Clock and took a shuttle back to our hotel where we were staying in the city of Niagara.

## The final day of the finale

That night, many more people arrived to hike with me the last day. This group included my sons, Ben and Lucas, and a bunch of their friends. These newcomers would join most of the people who hiked the first day.

We began at the Floral Clock and headed to the finish line of the falls.

As it makes the dramatic plunge off the escarpment, the water of the Niagara carries with it a tremendous amount of energy. This force had been converted to mechanical power as early as the mid-1700s. It was here in the late 1800s, though, that it was used to create electricity and the solution to transmitting electricity over a long distance was finally solved.

Today, we live in a world crisscrossed with power lines, most of which we hardly notice. But back then in the late 19th century, the idea that electricity could be generated in one place and used miles away smacked of magic.

So, if you needed some electric magic back then, whom would you consult? If you answered Thomas Edison, that's a good guess.

If you answered Nikola Tesla, even better.

Edison was a brilliant marketer, but Tesla was the better scientist and visionary. Edison thought that direct current (DC) was the mode in which electricity should be generated and transmitted. Tesla, on the other hand, patented motors and transformers designed to handle alternating current (AC).

In Niagara, Tesla won the debate, and when the Niagara Falls Power Company went online in 1894, they generated AC power, transmitting it over high-voltage lines to the city of Buffalo over twenty miles away where it was transformed back to a usable voltage.

If Tesla had walked with me this final day (and there were rumors that some of his interests included time travel, so maybe he was trailing our group that day), he would have passed by two of the five power plants now generating electricity from this falling water. The plant across the river from the path we walked, the Robert Moses Niagara Hydroelectric Power Station, is the largest. It houses 13 turbines and can generate 2.4 million kilowatts. This number would have seemed magical even to Tesla.

Much of the water used to create energy is now diverted from the falls. At least 60% is shunted through power plants today. At night and during the winter months when tourists are not flocking to see the falls, up to 75% is diverted. If this strikes you as unfortunate – maybe you want to see all that water thundering over the escarpment – consider this: the falls erode because of the force of all that water, so by diverting its force we are not only generating clean energy, but also slowing the upstream movement of the falls.

At that little art museum by the river, I saw a painting of the Horseshoe Falls from the early 1700s. I was amazed at how straight the falls were back then, lacking the signature arc. I wondered if the artist had smoothed out the horseshoe curve of the falls for his interpretation, but the rest of the painting seemed so literal that I looked into it. Indeed, the historical account and geological evidence show that the falls were barely curved back in the early 1700s. If you look at the falls today and draw a straight line across from edge to edge of outer points of the Horseshoe Falls, then move that line downriver around a hundred yards, this is where the edge of the escarpment stood three hundred years ago.

## The final steps

On the final day, I mingled with the group as we walked toward the falls, chatting with everyone and taking photos of people, the path, and the deep river gorge. We took a short break at the overlook at the whirlpool in the river. Here, the river takes a ninety-degree jog, and the racing water swirls and froths as it makes the abrupt turn. The walls of the river gorge plunge over two hundred feet down to the raging river. In places the walls of the gorge are sheer vertical rock; in others the angle has gentled, and trees hold their places where they can. A couple of people down in the gorge stood on giant boulders along the edge of the violent water. They looked like miniatures and I feared for their safety so near the raging waters. A historic cable car floated over this area, carrying tourists who wanted to hover over the rapids and whirlpool. A powerful jet boat raced upstream and into the whirlpool – the only type of watercraft that can withstand the pounding of the rapids – thrilling the people onboard.

We continued walking the trail, then, when we were two miles from the finish line at the falls, I began walking faster than the group. I desired to return to my usual pace when hiking, to find that natural gear once again, to feel the path move beneath me.

This was a moment for me to think back along the hundreds of miles I had covered this year, the five Great Lakes I had touched, the many connections between these inland seas I had hiked. I had walked path and road, rock and sand, marsh and swamp and bog, in two countries. I had seen the earth split open or tunneled to extract limestone and gypsum, sandstone and copper. I had seen raging rivers diverted to generate electricity. I had seen the ravages of urban decay, but also revitalization on riverfronts.

I had flowed with these waters for a time and listened to their voices as they moved with a gentle caress or thundered in waves that pounded insistently onto the shores. I had mingled with wildlife living on the edges of the largest freshwater system on earth.

I paused underneath the Peace Bridge that leaps across the river gorge connecting the two countries separated by – their edges defined by – the Niagara River. Light rain fell from the gray sky. From the vantage point underneath the bridge, I could see the American Falls. The mist drifted toward me, saturating the air with moisture, condensing on my glasses. The rest of the group, those who chose not to hike today, began to assemble at the visitor center near the finish line to greet the hiking group at the cusp of the Horseshoe Falls. I called them to say we were only 30 minutes away.

And then I paused.

The hikers with me had spread out a bit on the trail, and so they join me underneath the shelter of the bridge in small groups. I smile as I watch the group gather again. How wonderful that people would take time out of their lives to be part of this journey, to share these final steps with me, to give a cheer at the end. Excitement builds as we stand underneath the bridge, listening to the echo of the falling waters just upstream. When everyone catches up and we take a last few minute's rest, we set out as a group toward the finish.

We hike the final mile along the broad brick pathway that stretches along the river from the bridge to the falls. This is the area most heavily traversed by tourists, and we can walk three or four people abreast at times on the widening path. The whoosh of the American Falls is soon overtaken by the deeper, thundering roar of the Horseshoe Falls as we progress. People from all over the world walk nearby, having come to Niagara to see these waters take the famous plunge over the escarpment, and we hear fractured conversations in many different languages as we walk.

As we hikers near the Horseshoe Falls, the rest of our group forms a semi-circle to greet us. The hikers slow their pace, allowing me to emerge into the space between the hikers and the greeters.

If I am alone in that moment, it is only by a matter of a few feet, a few seconds, with friends and family within sight, within a few strides. I look down at my boots connecting with the bricks on the walkway for those final steps.

People begin to clap and cheer as the two groups converge with me at the center. I lift my arms above my head, lofting my walking stick as they come together.

At the end of my 1,000-Mile Great Lakes Walk, I am encircled and embraced by all.

# Epilogue

We shall not cease from exploration
And the end of all our exploring
Will be to arrive where we started
And know the place for the first time. . . .
– T.S. Eliot

This adventure was completed in the fall of 2012. On the shores of the Great Lakes, I found myself renewed. In the solitude of the hike I again found my center and strength. Day after day of walking sharpened my perceptions. Moving at three miles per hour under my own efforts, under the constant weight of my pack, became the new normal. Existing outdoors all day, and staying outside many nights, replaced my mostly indoor life. Wind, rain, and snow . . . heat, humidity and hail were ways I connected to the world with complete sensory immersion.

By moving through the land, I felt joined to migrations of the past. The Great Lakes were formed by a series of massive ice sheets that plowed down from the arctic, encasing the entire region in a towering sheet of ice. All living creatures had to migrate south as the walls of ice encroached on the land. Many creatures still migrate to survive: birds in particular, and even the fragile monarch butterfly. By walking day after day, I tapped in to that ancient compulsion to move through the land.

These waters speak to me. The geology tells me the story of how these lakes came to be. In taking time to listen and explore, I came to a deeper understanding of these vast inland seas. These waters restored and reshaped me. They broke me down and then rebuilt me so I now feel even more like myself than before.

That may sound strange, *How can you be more you?* Consider this: by stripping away possessions to only what I could carry in my pack, I redefined what was truly needed; by being alone for long periods, there was no one to form an opinion about me except myself; by being quiet – often not talking for days – I learned to be still and to observe, to breathe, and to simply listen.

There is something about the natural world that feeds a primal part of me . . . of us.

It is restorative.

One of my favorite quotes from John Muir is engraved on pillars at the Indiana Dunes State Park.

> *The Winds will blow their own freshness into you*
> *and the Storms their energy,*
> *while cares will drop off like autumn leaves.*

I cannot say it any better than that.

I encourage you to venture forth, to find your place – a place you will cherish and strive to protect – a place that speaks to you where your *cares will drop off like autumn leaves.*

Be it for a mile or a hundred or a thousand, walk that path to explore, expand, and experience.

I assure you that you will be more your true self for doing so.

Life *should* be an adventure.

# Acknowledgements

An adventure of 1,000 miles is not accomplished without assistance. I am in debt to many people who allowed me to ask questions, cheered me on, transported me to the lake, walked by my side, housed me along the way, or gathered in Niagara Falls, Ontario, for the finale of this grand adventure.

Thank you to the experts who took the time to enlighten me about Great Lakes issues: Kim Kaufman, Executive Director of the Black Swamp Bird Observatory; John Hartig, Manager of the International Wildlife Refuge near Detroit; Dr. Mike Hansen at the Hammond Bay Biological Research Center; and Drs. Bunnell, Madenjian, and Riley at the Great Lakes Research Center in Ann Arbor. I conducted formal interviews with these experts, and quotes in this book are from my notes. Casual conversations are related as I remember them.

Several people helped to shuttle me to and from the lakeshore, including Leslie, Milene, and Phil. Thanks also to Maija for giving me a lift and to several people who shortened a day here and there by driving me a few miles. In addition, I am thankful to those who took the time to read early versions or parts of this manuscript and to give thoughtful comments. Much gratitude to Theresa, Leslie, and Maija.

For the two-day finale hike from Niagara-on-the-Lake to Niagara Falls, many friends (old and new) and family walked by my side or greeted me at the falls for the final steps. A huge thanks to everyone who traveled to Niagara Falls to be part of the finale of this adventure. I will forever remember that moment when you encircled my final steps at the cusp of the falls.

Crickhollow Books under the direction of Philip Martin has been the best of homes for these books about my Great Lakes adventures.

# Bookstores on My Route

I encourage readers to support their local independent bookstores. These are special places where literature, regionalism, and community come together to celebrate where we live and what we care about. The success of my first book is due in large part to independent bookstores embracing the work and telling their communities about it.

These are the stores along my hiking route this time:

The Book Exchange, Port Clinton, OH

Great Northern Books and Hobbies, Oscoda, MI
Log Mark Bookstore, Cheboygan, MI
Falling Rock Café and Bookstore, Munising, MI
The Bookstore, Frankfort, MI
Dog Ears Books, Northport, MI
Brilliant Books, Traverse City, MI
The Cottage Book Shop, Glen Arbor, MI
The Island Bookstore, Mackinaw City & Mackinaw Island, MI
Between the Covers Bookstore, Harbor Springs, MI
McLean & Eakin Booksellers, Petoskey, MI
The Bookstore, Manistee, MI

Furby House Books, Port Hope, ON, Canada
Greenley's Bookstore, Belleville, ON, Canada

In addition, these bookstores have been strong supporters of my first book and deserve your support.

Unabridged Bookstore, Chicago, IL
Women & Children First, Chicago, IL
The Bookworks, Chicago, IL

Sandmeyer's Bookstore, Chicago, IL
57th Street Books, Hyde Park, IL
Powells, Hyde Park, IL
Quimby's, Chicago, IL
Barbara's Bookstore, Chicago, IL
Book Stall at Chestnut Court, Winnetka, IL
Lake Forest Bookstore, Lake Forest, IL

Forever Books, St. Joseph, MI
Black River Books, South Haven, MI
Readers World, Holland, MI
The Bookman, Grand Haven, MI
Book Nook & Java Shop, Montague, MI
Horizon Books, Traverse City, MI
Book World, St. Ignace, MI
Frigate Books, Gladstone, MI

Bayshore Books, Oconto, WI
LaDeDa Books & Beans, Manitowoc, WI

# Organizations
## Working to Protect the Great Lakes

These are some of the leading organizations working to protect the Great Lakes. They are worthy of your support, and they can assist you in understanding the complex challenges facing our Great Lakes.

Individually, we can do only a little; together, we can make a real difference in the health of the Great Lakes for us, our children, and future generations.

Alliance For the Great Lakes
  http://greatlakes.org

Black Swamp Bird Observatory
  http://www.bsbobird.org

Great Lakes Echo
  http://greatlakesecho.org

Great Lakes United
  http://www.glu.org

Healthy Lakes.org
  http://www.healthylakes.org

Sierra Club
  http://www.sierraclub.org

# Related Reading

Brzys, Karen A. *Agates Inside Out*. Grand Marais: Gitche Gumee Museum, 2010.

Berton, Pierre. *Niagara: A History of the Falls*. Albany: State U of NY Press, 1992.

Cheney, Margaret. *Tesla: A Man Out of Time*. New York: Simon & Schuster, 1981.

Dennis, Jerry. *The Windward Shore: A Winter on the Great Lakes*. Ann Arbor: University of Michigan Press, 2011.

Grady, Wayne. *The Great Lakes: The Natural History of a Changing Region*. Vancouver: Greystone Books, 2007.

Hall, Ed Y. *Harriet Quimby: America's First Lady of the Air*. Spartanburg: Honoribus Press, 1997.

Hartig, John. *Burning Rivers: Revival of Four Urban Industrial Rivers that Caught Fire*. Multi-Science Publishing Company, 2010.

Howard, Hugh. *Mr. And Mrs. Madison's War: America's First Couple and the Second War of Independence*. New York: Bloomsbury, 2012.

Lehto, Steve. *Michigan's Columbus: the Life of Douglass Houghton*. Royal Oak: Momentum, 2009.

Poling, Jim. *Tecumseh: Shooting Star, Crouching Panther*. Toronto: Dundurn, 2009.

Rowan Fasquelle, Ethel. *When Michigan was Young*. AuTrain: Avery Color Studios, 1991. (out of print)

Weeks, George. *Sleeping Bear: Yesterday & Today*. Ann Arbor: University of Michigan Press, 2005.

# Additional Links

**Videos from my adventures**

    http://YouTube.com/LNiewenhuis

**Lake Trek blog, author website, Facebook page**

Here are some links for news, book-related events, author talks, etc.

    The blog of my adventure with many photos is at:
    http://LakeTrek.Blogspot.com

    Author website: http://LakeTrek.com

    Facebook Author Page: http://Facebook.com/LakeTrek

**Recommended Artwork**

    Steve Brimm Photography
    http://www.SteveBrimm.com

    Sally Thompson
    http://sallythompson.stepanic.net

**Favorite B&Bs**

I sought out B&Bs along my route because owners of these unique and often historic houses are always knowledgeable about their communities and the history of the areas in which they live. Much of my research was informed by conversations with these gracious hosts along the lakeshores and by poking around many of their libraries.

    Please check the sidebar of my blog (http://LakeTrek.blogspot.com) for links to my favorite B&Bs along my route.

# Statistics from this Adventure

| | |
|---|---|
| Number of miles total: | 1,004 miles |
| Days on Trek: | 76 days |
| Average miles/day: | 13 miles |
| Longest day: | 27 miles |
| Percent of trek walked alone: | 92 % |
| Number of pairs of boots worn: | 2 pair |

Longest Segment:
Bay City, MI, to Harbor Springs, MI        303 miles in 22 days

Islands explored:
South Bass Island (Put-in-Bay), Grosse Isle, Mackinaw Island, North and South Manitou Islands